Diamythologōmen

Other books by Mark Anderson

Thinking Life: A Philosophical Fiction
Zarathustra Stone: Friedrich Nietzsche in Sils-Maria
Moby-Dick *as Philosophy: Plato-Melville-Nietzsche*

DIAMYTHOLOGŌMEN

A Philosophical Portrait of a Philosopher Philosophizing

Mark Anderson

S.Ph. Press

S.Ph. Press
Nashville, TN

Copyright © 2019 by S.Ph. Press

All rights reserved. No part of this publication may be reproduced or utilized in any form or by any means without permission in writing from the publisher.

ISBN-13: 978-0-9967725-7-0
ISBN-10: 0-9967725-7-X

Library of Congress Control Number: 2018909933

www.sphpress.com

Table of Contents

1. *Sum, ergo cogito* — 1
2. *Ti esti philosophia?* — 14
3. The creek and the cloud — 36
4. *Philia* and *sophia* — 54
5. *Regressus ad infinitum* — 69
6. Thinking life — 87
7. Thought and world — 111
8. Notes on Plato and Nietzsche — 131
9. *Primavera* — 182

Live madly when young; later, soberly but creatively. Be serious about your education. Study and learn to appreciate the undisputed important books, and the great works of art; master your pleasures and pains, your particular temptations and fears; train yourself in elegance and nobility of character; cultivate an amiable independence. Experience. Mature. *Think*.

Then relax, and believe and do whatever moves you. In brief, trust the inclinations of a refined subjectivity. There may be nothing more to *sophia* and *eudaimonia* than this. If there is, it will come to you. — Michael Tommasi

Sum, ergo cogito

Oh, should've worn my jacket. Not too cold though. The walk'll warm me up. And beautiful. The sky. The leaves. Autumn morning. Autumnal mood.

"Buongiorno, Scialla! Come va? Stai bene? Hai dormito bene? Brava! Brava, Sciallina! Fa bel tempo, vero? A little cold, però è bello. Allora, facciamo due passi? A walk down Oakland to Belmont? Sì, dai, let's go!"

Empty streets, good. Rising red sun, nostalgic chill. Once as a child cresting Robin Hill Road I looked out on a rolling wood beyond. Miles away but looming. Multi-colored depths blazing, chiaroscuro afternoon. Years gone. Home long gone. I love a sidewalk overhung with trees and blanketed with leaves, melancholic though it is. Like a trellised arbor-way into another time, another world. *Augenblick*. All things from their opposites.

...

Luminous October morning sky, pink cloud banks, red leaves repose. Morning chill, October blue, singular leaf—red-leaf repose. Still a little cold though, but not uncomfortable. Anyway not unbearable. It's bracing. Invigorating air, shimmering dawn. Brick-brown leaves release, decline, settle on the grass to sleep. To dream.

Let the dream be. Let the myth be. Against interpretation. Nostalgia is merely unsatisfied desire, he says. I think it's better altogether to avoid *merely* here. Subtleties and complications, reverberating nuances of depth.

But to what end, nostalgia?

But must it be oriented toward a *telos*? Must there be a single specific aetiology? Rather, free-floating melancholy infused with cognitive content. Luminous October morning blue. An underground river. Chill. Surfacing at intervals.

Odysseus's nostalgia was geographical, proceeding through the present toward home. Ours is temporal, a fruitless longing for the past. Backward-willing. Homelessness. Recurrent suffering's a brute fact, the periodic ache, to which we provide a meaning through interpretation, the imposition of form. Nostalgia, for example.

'Come back, come back, O glittering and white!'

A fantasy figure lingers out of sight, around a corner of my lost city, behind a streetlamp on the sidewalk of my youth. Gas flame. Iridescent fog. *Augenblick*.

Oh, this guy. Every morning. Alright, here he comes.

"Aspetta, Scialla, aspetta. Siedeti. Sit, Scialla, sit. Stay. Stai qui. Sì, brava… Morning. Fine, thanks… Brava Scialla! Va bene, andiamo."

Interruptions out of my head, attention diverted to my body limbs the external world. Sensory receptors, noise and movement, stimulation excitation of nerves. I experience, even *feel*, the focused awareness drain from the pit of my mind, rush into my eyes skin and fingertips. From the depths to the surface, so easy to be dragged out of thought.

And how to dive back in?

Nostalgia as lamenting the divide between the world's abundance and the limits of one's experience. Andy says. Nostalgia epistemic. The longing to feel more than one can feel, be more than one is. Capacious. Oh, I'm back in it

Sum, ergo cogito

now. To encompass the contraries and contradictions. To see everything as it is, infinite.

Or not. As it is not.

O glittering and white! Glimmering? Glittering. Glittering? Again, nostalgia as this or that interpretation of a gloom in itself unspecified and undirected. 'I maintain the phenomenality of the inner world, too.' Interpretation as falsification, even of the self. So-called 'self.'

One's spiritual atmosphere autumnal dawn. Unaccountable mood. Is it Fall or fall? Lower-case *f*, I think. A smile for the transient, Being's glow settling on Becoming. Neither true nor false, good nor bad. *Augenblick*.

The problem of the internal world. Epiphenomenon of what, exactly? What's going on in there? Down there. Flickering illumination, shadows on the wall. The cave in the mind and the self as Theseus, as the labyrinth too, and sometimes as the Minotaur.

"Tutto bene? Fai la brava, Sciallina? Sì, così sei brava."

Socrates has no time to naturalize the myths. Clever sophistical explanations. Reductive rationalizations. He wants to know himself. γνῶθι σαυτόν. Delphi. Apollo god of light. Reason pilot of the soul. Is he a hundred-headed beast or a simple thing with a share in the divine?

But these too are mythological, fantastical conceptions.

For a god to command that a mortal know himself is devious cruel. Dry leaves on the wind, the stirring of winter, stirring of soul. Knowledge is out of reach, and anyway not the objective. Let the myth be. The old man has regrets, longs for return, reunion, the final spiritual homecoming. Reclining by the river, under the trees, barefoot on

Diamythologōmen

the grass evokes the state. The mood. Pray Pan we may be good.

More fantasy, that. Pan and goodness both. Socrates too.

Reason equals virtue equals happiness. Through the proper activity of intellect, of clear, precise, logical cogitation, one intuits the true the good the beautiful and then, believing the true, doing the good, admiring the beautiful—*e voilà!* One is happy. Prudent, upright, content. These people really should rake their leaves. The good man and true, splendid to behold, at peace and free of pain, physical and psychic. Reason equals virtue equals happiness. The cure for ills, for melancholia. Align your subjectivity with the nature of the real.

Nostalgia for the truth.

Objectivism. The evasion of objectivism. Subjective genitive. *Objectivism as evasion*. It's not me; it's the world. The hierarchy of being and value. It's not me; it's the world.

"Basta, Scialla! Basta! Stai calma."

Let the dream be, work its magic, which it'll do on its own if we resist the urge to interpret it. No need to translate reveries into a foreign tongue, the vocabulary of reason. Even symbolism. The dream employs its own peculiar idiom. Infuses the spirit, colors the soul in the image of its moods. Brick-brown, brown penny.

"Scialla, basta! Calm down now!"

I think, and the dream manifest of a thought-world envelops the images and words. An essentializing steam enforming matter. (οὐσία) Seeps inside infusing, instills meaning, reifies.

Sum, ergo cogito

But substance is a fiction, and the atom is a shadow of the old God.

God, it's still just a little too cold. And snowfall's a month away, at least. Oh Scialla, basta!

"Ascolta, Scialla. Basta! Adesso basta! Mi senti? Dio, Scialla! Dio mio!"

...

Relax, breathe...

...

I wrote: I believe there is... I believe there may well be an objective hierarchy of being and value, and that to attain our proper good we must align ourselves with it—must align our souls, must, must align ourselves with it. I believe moreover that if there is such a hierarchy, it's likely best expressed in the Platonic tradition. Philosophy as training for dying and being dead. Purification.

But I also believe that possibly none of this is so, that Nietzsche's critique of these and related traditions is sound, and his perspective in general plausible and appealing.

I incline toward the one or the other perspective depending on my mood. Sometimes a Platonist. Sometimes a Nietzschean. Always both.

Or neither—*contra* doctrine, anti-isms. The man before the system.

I also suspect that even if one aligns oneself with the real objective hierarchy of being and value, still this doesn't secure happiness. Eudaimonia's maybe just a word. Wisdom too.

It really is a bizarre equation, reason equals virtue equals happiness.

Also wisdom = knowledge.

Socrates and Aristotle believed these things, maybe. Probably. Plato I think was beyond good and evil, belief and unbelief. The man who has control of himself has no need for beliefs about the true the good or the beautiful.

"Vero, Scialla? Sì! E ora stai tranquilla. Brava! Brava, Sciallina!"

Being is said in many ways, but 'I see nothing other than becoming.' I love these trees even as they shed their skin, as nature as an ancestor, progenitor, source and cessation of wandering. Repose in the comforting blur of Being. To disappear, to come home. Nostalgia not for death or pre-existence, but for life as pure potential, lingering in the anteroom, innocent anticipation.

But this is the opposite of capacious. Suffering evinces a constricted perspective, Blake's narrow chinks. Right? Flight from pain, to correct being, to declare it all unreal. *Hinterwelten*. Beyond-worlds. So many modes of evasion.

'Come back, come back, O glittering and white!'

Nostalgic for the experience of nostalgia. When Greece had the power to evoke the Greeks. When I had the spirit to find the Greeks in Greece. Walking naked the Heraion stoa I encountered the ghosts of Kelobis and Biton, counting no man happy before he dies. History haunted Argolid. But that was years ago. Today in Athens the Ilisos is overgrown, the shrines along its banks effaced from time. No frolicking girls, divine winds, no poetry or philosophy. Only the highway hum of traffic, smut and smog and grey sludge, abandoned dogs and men.

That bird.

"Cosa c'è, Scialla? Un uccellino? Sì, ma guarda lì! Guarda gli scoiattoli. The squirrels! See?! Vedi? Sì, sei brava! Oh Dio! Sono veloci, vero? Ha! Brava! Brava, Sciallina!"

...

He says, 'My music is the spiritual expression of what I am.' This is true of philosophy, of science, of religion and myth, of any comprehensive engagement with life, any composition of a thought-world.

Yet we deny it.

It's not me; it's the world.

The music shapes character—when the ways of music change, laws change—and the character shapes the music, and cultural patterns shape these, and these shape culture, and trends of thought, down even to the deepest strata of perception and logical structure, shape and are shaped by all this, and so on. These forces merge in various overlapping and mutually interpenetrating ways, a web of continuity of active interacting influences.

Truth is the whole, the manifold, the all. And the One is the Many, the many the one, being and becoming.

But we, we isolate that specific particular among the plurality which we prefer, which for various existential, psychological, pragmatic or aesthetic reasons we prefer, are drawn to or at ease with, moved by or ennobled by, and then through sophistic appeals to evidence or argument we contend that *this* is the cause of all the others, the source of

Diamythologōmen

their being or activity, not vice versa or according to any other order of dependence.

But it's all mythology.

In philosophy too. *This* is the central node from which all else radiates. *This* is fundamental. *This* is substance. God. The singular truth.

Ah, now, finally I'm warm.

We won't want to walk mornings when winter comes. But snowfall's still a month away, at least. If it snows at all.

We justify, defend, excuse, evade the subjectivity of our own experience and judgment. But really we aren't after proof, rather plain persuasion, of self and others. We crave fellow-feeling, company and affirmation. Permission to be ourselves. We insist our aim is that our thoughts correspond to the real. To speak as a mouthpiece of the beyond. τὰ ὄντα. It's the pretense of ontology. In fact our truth is rhetorical flourish, the intellectual residue of falsehoods become conventional, melted snow. Truth drops out and reflective equilibrium, warranted assertibility, or inference to the best—to the plausible—to me, to my own subjectivity—it's the best we ever get. Justification by our own lights. The web of belief. And our *physis* is *nomos* to its roots, *logos* sprung from *mythos*.

Or so it appears to me now. Ha!

The mask of objectivism. *It's not me! It's the world!*

The fancy of the real. *It's not me! It's the world!*

"Il mondo, Scialla. Vero? Non noi; il mondo. Noi siamo bravi, vero? Ha! Magari!"

...

Sum, ergo cogito

God, I imagine these trees would speak to me, or are me speaking. To myself. Projections of the psyche I mistake for external objects, independently existent things. (In which case *you* should rake your *own* leaves!) Or maybe the mistake runs the opposite way and 'I' am really just the world, falsely perceiving and conceiving me as independent of itself. The self as nature contemplating nature as a field of symbols, of signs—no, of it knows not what. Even what it appears to be as mysterious as what it is, or rather might be, assuming it's anything at all.

Which it isn't.

Or is.

And if nature itself is manifest through divine self-contemplation, a self-reflective self-portrait of the One? Then I'm at a third remove from the real, the dream of a dream. Plato's least real artifact, least valuable. And what then about my intellect, my reason?

Unreasonable.

Including even this chain of reasoning?

Looped in the loops of a brown-penny mind.

Infinite self-reflection.

And Plato, I think, was unwell...

...

Well, and the Buddha replied that *that* is the greatest possible question and *this* is the greatest possible answer.

The greatest? That and this, and—

So: Is there a problem of the universe, and, if so, what is it, and what is the solution?

Yes, and that was it, and this is the solution.

Diamythologōmen

Wait.

Is there a problem of the universe, and, if so, what is it, and what is the solution?

Yes, and that was it, and this is the solution.

Alright, so:

One: Yes, there is a problem of the universe.

Two: The problem of the universe is: Is there a problem of the universe, and, if so, what is it, and what is the solution?

Three: The Solution is: Yes, there is a problem of the universe, and that (two) was it, and this (three) is the solution.

Is there a problem of the universe, and, if so, what is it, and what is the solution?

The problem of the universe is the problem whether there is a problem of the universe; and the solution is, yes, *that*.

Is there a problem of the universe? Yes.

What is it? Is there a problem of the universe?

What's the solution? All this.

So, yes, there is a problem of the universe, namely *the problem whether there is a problem of the universe, and, if so, what that problem is, and what the solution is*, and the solution is that 'yes, there is a problem of the universe, namely *the problem whether there is a problem of the universe, and, if so, what that problem is, and what the solution is.*'

The problem is: Is there a problem? The solution is: Yes, this, all this.

The problem is: Is there a problem? The solution is: Yes.

Sum, ergo cogito

Damn! Is that—I'm lost, looped—I'm, and the infinite regress is a manifestation in miniature of the problem...

Is there a problem of the universe, and, if so, what is it, and what is the solution?

Yes, and that was it, and this is the solution.

Is there a problem of the universe, and, if so, what is it, and what is the solution?

Yes, there is a problem of the universe, namely *the problem whether there is a problem of the universe, and, if so, what that problem is, and what the solution is*, and the solution is that 'yes, there is a problem of the universe, namely *the problem whether there is a problem of the universe, and, if so, what that problem is, and what the solution is.*'

The problem is: Is there a problem? The solution is: Yes.

Yes, there is a problem.

Yes. A problem.

Enough!

"Basta! Vero, Scialla? Let's just relax. We're walking. Just thinking. Relax."

...

The peculiar vice of the thinking man: (The problem) He mistakes what seems to him good, for himself here and now, for what really is good, in and of itself, for everyone, at all times and everywhere.

The evasion of objectivism.

Yes, there is a problem.

Basta! Drop it already. Move on.

We inflate our temporary moods into essential character, and this into the human as such.

The mask. The pose.

Diamythologōmen

The problem.

But why dispute about these things? (The universe) Why argue, even with myself? As if truth were at stake.

Maybe it is. Something is.

Either it or I.

Or I and it.

All things from their opposites. The problem of the—

Augenblick.

Against the hierarchy of being and value. A fabrication! Against interpretation. Fiction! And 'why not rather untruth,' all the way down?

The agitation caused by disagreement is often worse than the agitation that caused the disagreement. The agitation caused by arguing is worse than the agitation—worse than that which caused the argument. If I win the argument, does that prove I'm right? If you win, does that prove you're right? Let's leave these things to their endless permutations, leap into the boundless and there live out our days.

Let's make our body like a withered tree, our mind like dead ashes. 'Free and easy wandering,' no distinctions no discriminations. Awash in the flow, can't step in the river one is the river.

Let's say Yes, then. Yes to the dream, yes to the years, yes to the truth and the lack thereof and yes to the I don't know. Luminous October morning blue. Yes! Nostalgic chill. Yes! And 'some day I wish to be only a Yes-sayer.'

We won't walk in a month when snow arrives. Oh, let's hope for snow and not just sleet and slush, on these sidewalks, on these streets. Damn, Nashville! You always do a winterman wrong!

Sum, ergo cogito

Our road. Turn right, cross the street.

"Qui giriamo a destra, Scialla. To the right. Sì, così. Brava! La nostra strada, vero? Siamo quasi a casa. Almost home, Sciallina. There's our house, vero? Sì, dai, andiamo!"

Socrates' dream, Socrates' death, it's Plato dreaming of Socrates dreaming. Plato as Prime Mover, demiurge of a thought-world.

Plato, practice *mousikê*! Cultivate your artistry!

Pondering man, walking in the garden.

Plato the poet.

Philosophy as art.

Living as thinking. Thinking as living.

Home.

"Eccoci qua, Scialla. Siamo arrivati."

Home?

Ti esti philosophia?

Professor: What is philosophy? Ha! Well, yes, that *is* the question, isn't it? And you know, Wyatt, I myself consider this the philosopher's central question, if not the central philosophical question. Anyway, looking back I realize that over the years some version of this has been my constant concern as a philosopher. What am I doing, how am I living, *as* a philosopher? And is *this* the proper mode of the philosophical life?

Now, for example, as we're speaking, am I living and acting as a philosopher? Or rather as a professor of philosophy? Or as some other type altogether? This matters to me, and to such an extent I'm inclined to say that the philosopher's perennial preoccupation centers on inquiring into himself as a philosopher. What *is* the philosophical life, and am I living it? Here and now, am I really living it?

Obviously, this is related to the matter of self-reflection and self-examination, the Delphic *gnôthi sauton*, Socrates' 'know thyself.' And so—but yeah, Wyatt, what is it?

Wyatt: Sorry to interrupt, but I'm wondering about that distinction between the philosopher's central question and the central philosophical question.

Professor: Ah, yes, well, I glossed right over that, didn't I? Ha! And with good reason—I spoke without considering exactly what I meant, or what I'd say if someone asked me about it. So thanks for complicating my morning, Wyatt!

But no, really, it's not the first time I've made the distinction. I make it often, in my head I mean. But whenever I do I'm troubled because, although it rings true, I've never taken sufficient time to work out, not even to my own satisfaction, the *precise* distinction I mean to identify here. So how about this: I'll say what I'm able to say about it now, in the moment, but with the caveat that I wouldn't insist on this as the best, or as my final, formulation of the matter. Will that work? Is that all right?

Wyatt: Yeah, sure, alright.

Professor: Ok, good. So. By the *philosophical* question I mean something like the paradigmatic question, the quintessentially all-encompassing question, the ur-question which in a way sums up the pursuit of philosophers throughout the ages. I'm thinking for example of a question like, 'What's the nature of ultimate reality?' Or, 'Is there a God, or anything like a conscious, intentional, and creative agent within, behind, or beyond the physical universe, and responsible for it as its cause?' Or, 'What is knowledge, what is truth, and is knowledge of the truth attainable?'

By the *philosopher's* question on the other hand I mean the question the sincere philosopher is compelled to ask himself, or herself, continually, ceaselessly, the question voiced alongside, and underneath, every other question, every philosophical question in particular. What exactly am I doing when I think about reality, god, and truth? Am I seeking wisdom, wisdom as knowledge? Am I exploring possibilities? Am I playfully creating? Am I inducing in myself a psychic mystification? Am I plunging into profundities, or rising to the sublime, or, well, you get the point—but in any case what exactly am I doing? In what mode does the philosopher, *qua* philosopher, engage with such matters, intellectually, existentially? And am I doing this, here and now? Am I addressing this philosophical question *as a philosopher*? Or, better: Am I *living* as a philosopher?

I don't know, does this make sense? As I said, I'm sure this isn't the clearest, or even the most accurate, way to express the distinction I have in mind, but I think it captures at least the gist of what I'm after. What do you think? Is this good for now?

Wyatt: Yeah, sure, thanks. I see what you're getting at, more or less. But the way you're putting it, it sounds almost obsessive, you know? I mean, should the philosopher really be so constantly concerned with probing himself and his motivations this way? Where's the peace, the zen, the tranquility of wisdom in all this? Shouldn't the philosopher just *be*, without all the frantic self-analysis?

Professor: Well, yeah, you're onto something there, Wyatt. Sure. I don't mean to suggest that the philosopher is given to excessive or morbid self-dissection, just that he, or she, is less concerned with the methodology of problem solving than with a style of living, and that this must be intentional. Philosophy as a way of life. It's a matter of priorities, right?

Wyatt: Yeah, that makes sense. And now I'm reminded of something I read, that the philosopher's aim is to understand how things fit together, in a broad sense of that expression. Or something like that. Do you know what I'm talking about? And is this related, or relevant here?

Professor: Ah, you're thinking of Wilfrid Sellars' line that the aim of philosophy is to understand how things, in the broadest possible sense of the term, hang together, in the broadest possible sense of the term. Vague as it is, it's a plausible idea. I mean, it covers a lot of ground, right? But for just that reason I doubt it's very helpful to our specific inquiry. For example, it doesn't really distinguish the philosopher from the scientist, does it?

But maybe you've hit on a helpful approach here, Wyatt. Consider the various proposals regarding the nature of philosophy. Definitions of the discipline. To begin with, for example, we might wonder whether it's appropriate to think of philosophy as a discipline. Is philosophy a field of study? Is it a profession? Is it a scholarly-historical pursuit, or an intellectual activity grounded in logic and allied with science? Is philosophy a *Wissenschaft*? Or is it rather a mode of intellectual creativity? Of free-spiritedness? Is it a spiritual condition? A way of life? A psychic and existential orientation? Toward what, exactly?

You see? If we want to know whether we're living and thinking as philosophers, it'll help if we have some idea what philosophy is. No? Problem is, it turns out that this is really hard.

Mary: So what about Quine's idea that philosophy of science is philosophy enough? If that's right, then philosophy isn't distinct from science after all. Or maybe it's distinct, because philosophy of science isn't science, but it's not so far removed as some would like to make it, and as you maybe just implied.

Tyler: Yeah, but there's also Quine's contention that all our beliefs are radically revisable, even including the axioms of logic, and that our observations are theory-laden to such an extent that physical objects are posits every bit as speculative as Homer's gods. I mean, the typical scientist seems to believe he's discovering the truth about the world, about reality as it is, whereas Quine regards science as our best instrument for negotiating the world of experience, but not as revealing the capital-T Truth, the *real* from a god's-eye point of view. In that sense Quine's an Instrumentalist or Pragmatist, I think. The web of belief and all that. But most scientists are naive realists, aren't they?

Professor: Well, on this matter I think we can say this, at least: your typical practicing scientist thinks differently about his enterprise than do many of the best philosophers of science. The scientists are far less self-reflective about the implications of their assumptions and commitments. Less informed. They fancy themselves empiricists, but most don't understand, as the philosophers do—and here I'm thinking of Hume and Quine in particular, but also of more recent figures like Bas van Fraassen and, more recently still, Kyle Stanford—anyway, the scientists don't understand that empiricism strictly speaking implies some version or other of anti-realism, phenomenalism, or skepticism.

If our information about the world—that's a problematic word here, *information*, but let's just go with it for now—if our information about the world comes only by way of impacts on our sensory receptors, then all we know directly are the phenomena of our immediate experience, with maybe some degree of legitimacy granted to memory, but at best we can only *infer* the existence of an external world, and this inference takes us beyond the evidence supplied by our senses—including, by the way, the question whether

Ti esti philosophia?

we really *are* equipped with sensory receptors to begin with, since our bodies are—or are supposed to be—objects in the external world, and therefore subject to the same inferential conditions as every other supposedly external object. So, in short, the world as studied by science is a theoretical construct underdetermined by the evidence. Even *radically* underdetermined, to the precise probability of zero.

Mary: So there's no point to science then? It's merely useful, and we can dismiss it as philosophically insignificant?

Professor: No, no, not at all. The fact that science is useful *is* significant, don't get me wrong. The activity of science—or rather of the sciences, plural, since there really is no singular, unified scientific method, as Feyerabend delighted in pointing out—the sciences instantiate the most efficient methods we've devised so far to intervene in and manipulate the empirical world. Whether for good or ill, ultimately, is another matter altogether, of course. Probably a more important matter, but we'll set that aside for now. In any case, the point I want to make is that this empirical world the sciences manipulate with such facility is a theoretical posit, as Tyler said—as he correctly said that Quine said—which for all we know is false, or neither true nor false because—again, for all we know—there's no objective nature of reality beyond the many posits to function as their measure. Or if there is some such reality, we have no access to it, which amounts to the same thing, practically speaking. So anyway, our truth, the so-called truths we're pleased to think we know about the empirical world, depend for their nature, and even for their very existence, on various undergirding posits, which are false, or arbitrary, or, at best, empirically accurate and theoretically fecund but, for all that, utterly unverifiable, even in theory.

So, no matter how useful science is in its practical applications, if it does not, and cannot, generate knowledge of truth, much less *exclusive* knowledge of the truth—

Tyler: Scientism!

Professor: Right. And the idea that science, and only science, can discover the truth about the world—well, let's just say it's an ironically *un*-scientific perspective. Basically, it's a bald metaphysical assumption unsupported, and unsupportable, by its own narrow standards of evidence. And by the way, one doesn't have to be a theist or a weak-minded metaphysician to reject scientism. Far from it. One could agree with all, or anyway most, of the nihilistic conclusions about reality propounded by Alex Rosenberg and still regard his childlike faith in science as philosophically naive, and suggestive of an impoverished imagination.

But anyway, if science isn't a source of knowledge of objective truth, then we can't appeal to the modern system of the world as the standard by which to judge competing world-views. Nor then can we look to science, or to science-oriented philosophers, for assistance in determining the proper mode and aim, or aims, of philosophy.

In short, philosophy of science might well be philosophy enough for those who aspire to think and live exclusively according to the timeliness of their time. But for those who refuse to confine their thinking to the presuppositions and conventionalities of any particular time and place, philosophy of science, as valuable as it is—and it *is* valuable, essential even; philosophers of science are responsible for some of the very insights we're working with here—as valuable as it is, philosophy of science is only one fine strand in the elaborate woven fabric of philosophy.

Tyler: So is skepticism the best we can hope for then, supplemented maybe with conventional standards and social agreements to negotiate the world? I mean, there has to be a standard for action, and maybe different standards for different fields of activity and forms of life, but some set or sets of standards, however malleable in the long run, if we're going to act at all.

Mary: All right, sure, but how do we decide on the standards? If, as was just said, there's a serious question whether what's good as science is good for the world, or for life, then the dispute over standards goes all the way down. There's no bedrock, no final appeal to decide the issue.

Tyler: Exactly! Skepticism, like I said!

Ryan: So isn't this, aren't we now getting to the problem of the criterion? Any standard to which we appeal to justify or ground an argument or assertion must itself be justified, and the standard that grounds this justification will have to be justified in turn, and so on. Right? Agrippa's trilemma.

Professor: Yeah, go on.

Ryan: Oh, ok. So, the trilemma. The standard or criterion invoked to ground an argument is, first, either hypothesized or baldly asserted, in which case it's unproven. Or, second, it can be proven only by the conclusion it's meant to prove, so it's a product of circular reasoning. Or, third, its proof depends on another standard which itself must be proven by a still different standard, which must be proven in its turn, and so on ad infinitum. In short, it's impossible to prove any assertion or to justify any argument because there's no fully and finally proven criterion on which to base any particular proof. So it's more skepticism, right?

Professor: Yes! And now we've arrived at Pyrrhonism. The ancient Pyrrhonians took the problem of the criterion so seriously they declined to assent to any impression as indicative of truth beyond the immediate appearances, the non-evident, as they called it. It appears to me now, for example, that I'm sitting in a room talking with other people, but whether this is really so or not, whether the world in itself is organized or constituted in this way, as a matter of objective fact, I don't know. This is non-evident. To other humans, to other animals, or even to myself in other circumstances or under different conditions, the appearances may differ, radically even. And maybe I'm insane or dreaming, or maybe I'm a brain in a vat.

Moreover, it also appears to me that at least some of the standard arguments against the independent reality of space and time, and even against objects, things, and thing-hood itself—I'm thinking now of Zeno, of Kant, of Nietzsche, or of contemporary so-called 'object nihilists' like Baptiste Le Bihan—it appears to me now that at least some of their arguments are sound, in which case my observations, my experiences of *things*, are at odds with my idea that things maybe don't exist. And if there's no independently and finally provable criterion to which to appeal to adjudicate these various disputes, then we ought to withhold our assent from any assertion about the way the world really is, in itself, independent of the appearances, or so the Pyrrhonians advised. And the word for this suspension of judgment is *epochê*. The Pyrrhonians counseled *epochê* as the proper response to disagreement and the problem of the criterion.

Tyler: But not exclusively for epistemological reasons, right? Their ultimate aim was peace of mind.

Christopher: *Ataraxia*! Freedom from agitation or mental disturbance. The Pyrrhonians were seeking *ataraxia*, right?

Professor: Right, yes, but with the accent on the penultima, on the 'iota.' Anyway, as Sextus tells the story, once there lived some ancient thinkers who hoped to attain *ataraxia* by discovering the truth. They were agitated by philosophical disagreement, and they reasoned that their agitation would vanish if they resolved the disagreements. But as it turned out, the disagreements were unresolvable, the truth of the matter impossible to discover, so they threw up their hands and abandoned the search as fruitless. And in that very moment, *voilà!*, they attained peace of mind, *ataraxia*.

Philosophy for the Pyrrhonians, then, was a form of spiritual therapy. A common orientation in the Hellenistic period. The Epicureans and the Stoics were aiming for certain intellectual, psychological, or spiritual conditions too, refined pleasure or a minimum of passions and emotions. In our own day, Wittgenstein regarded the task of philosophy as therapeutic, though perhaps in a different sense than the ancients had in mind. But in any case, we're confronting now different conceptions of both the nature and the goal of philosophy. Is the philosopher seeking to discover something outside herself, the truth? Or is she attempting to affect something within herself, goodness or happiness or tranquility? Or maybe both, the one by way of the other? But then again we might wonder whether the philosopher seeks anything at all. In which case we're back to the question regarding the philosopher's conception of philosophy as a mode of living and thinking.

Mary: So what about that line you like to quote about philosophy and conflicting interpretations of Plato?

Professor: Ah, yes, you're thinking of Seth Benardete's observation that the question of what philosophy is, is inseparable from the question of how to read Plato.

Wyatt: So dialectic then? Philosophy is the search for the truth of being—in essences, in the Forms—by way of dialectic?

Tyler: Yeah, but look, we're reading the *Phaedrus*, and we just read the *Ion*. Where's the dialectic in these dialogues? It's not there. Not anyway as described in the *Republic*.

Christopher: And not as illustrated in the *Sophist*.

Wyatt: So maybe dialectic in an informal sense, as conversation? The dialogues are at least conversations. I mean, what are Socrates and Phaedrus doing but talking?

Mary: But the central metaphysical tenets are disclosed in a speech, a speech it seems we're supposed to take as divinely inspired, even as an expression of god-given madness.

Professor: Yes, a madness that's a 'divine release from customary usages' and a 'withdrawal from human pursuits.' And this recalls the account in the *Phaedo* of the living separation of soul from body, the spirit's withdrawal from the interests, concerns, and distractions of the body to

Ti esti philosophia?

gather itself together with itself. In the *Phaedo*—which we'll read next semester—in the *Phaedo* this separation from the body is called *purification*. It's a central theme of the work, and it figures in the *Phaedrus* too, remember, when Socrates delivers his second speech explicitly as an act of purification, a *katharsis*.

Tyler: But isn't purification itself a therapeutic end? And doesn't the content of the *Phaedo* suggest that this is Plato's aim for the philosopher?

Professor: In a sense, yeah, I think that's right. But maybe we'd better not speak of *Plato's* aim. Let's speak instead of 'Platonism,' or even of something else, something like, 'a prominent strand running through some of Plato's dialogues.' This is fair I think. But in any case, yes, therapeutic. Knowledge or wisdom leads to, or includes, or maybe it just *is*, aligning one's intellect, character, and soul with the objective hierarchy of being and value—the true, the good, and the beautiful—and, as I say, this alignment produces, or just is, the healthy condition of the soul, the soul healed of the corruptions that infect it in and through embodied life.

Wyatt: So then Platonism really does involve seeking knowledge of the truth? For therapeutic purposes, sure, but still the therapy works only if there is this hierarchy of being and value, an objective standard, a truth.

Professor: Yeah, I think that's right. But, as I say, it's right about a certain strand running through some of the dialogues. And, look, I'm sure this belief in objective truth is an expression of certain tendencies in Plato himself, in his spirit, by which I mean his instincts and habits of thinking and living. Still, as significant and real as this may be, in Plato's dialogues and in his person, it doesn't encompass the entirety of the work, and it certainly doesn't encompass the man. If anything, the man encompasses the work, as its creator. And therefore he encompasses, and expands beyond, his characters' frequent concern with being and truth. Plato is ontologically prior to all this, and spiritually more capacious.

Christopher: All right, but all we have of the man are the dialogues. And even then it's clear he's hiding himself in, or behind, his work.

Professor: No doubt he is, in a sense. But in another sense he's revealing himself, revealing aspects of himself he doesn't reveal in the explicit content of the dialogues. And I mean aspects of himself *as a philosopher*. Look, when thinking about the dialogues it's good to keep in mind that Plato is the only actual, actually living, philosopher on display in them, or rather *through* them. Everyone else is a character of his invention. Even the real, historical figures— as characters in his work they're conjurings of his creative power. And so they're subject to his artist's laws. In short, the dialogues are spiritual expressions, in the broadest sense of the term, of Plato himself.

Christopher: Or spiritual expressions of his hiding.

Professor: Yeah, that may be. But that too would provide a revelation of the man, insight into his spirit as a philosopher. And maybe we could connect this to the stress on covering and uncovering, hiding and revelation, at the conclusion of the *Phaedo*—some of you know what I mean by this. Tyler, you know. There's no need to go into it now though. If you haven't yet read the *Phaedo*, you'll see next semester. In any case, as Nietzsche wrote, Platonism's a frightening mask behind which hides some great thing. And I suspect this great thing is Plato himself, Plato as something greater than any single character in his dialogues, greater even than the sum of all the characters, and even including their broader dramatic contexts. In the dialogues we encounter Plato the thinker. But *through* them we discover Plato the artist. And like most great artists Plato has among his many facets a flash of Magritte's, 'I don't want to solve a mystery. I want to create one.'

So, yes, Plato hides himself behind his revelations. But he reveals himself through his hidings too. It's covering and uncovering all the way down.

Wyatt: So, what, it's not standard to figure Plato's artistry into accounts of his nature as a philosopher? I mean, he wrote dialogues, which would seem at least to call attention to his preferred method of communication. There's a writerly quality to his work unique among philosophers, right? Seems like something we shouldn't just ignore.

Christopher: But we've read some scholars who've noted the significance of Plato as a writer. But you complained they got him wrong anyway.

Professor: Yeah, that's right. Of course there are those who write at length about Plato as a stylist, and who acknowledge and appreciate the poetry of his prose—you'll recall the essays we read by Dorothy Tarrant and Helen Bacon. And some scholars recognize, and even insist, that Plato's choosing to write, and to write in the way he did, is essential to our understanding of his conception of philosophy. I'm thinking now of Frede, Sayre, and Rowe, to name just those whose work we've read. Yet these and a select few other scholars, as serious as they are—and they are serious, and very much worth learning from—still, they tend to view Plato's writing through the lens of their own experience with authorship, namely as scholars and professional academics. When *they* write, they write to make a point, to persuade the reader of a particular thesis, or to contribute to our collective store of learning, and—and perhaps primarily—to *teach*. So, generally, whatever they say about Plato as a writer, they're still inclined to see him as a teacher, a teacher of dialectic, and they regard his writing ultimately as one of his modes of teaching.

Here's the thing, the problem with the scholar as a type is that he understands only the words and characters *on* the page. He has no feel for the author *behind* the page. This is so because whatever the scholar *writes* on the page, whatever he says *in* his text, is precisely what he means to *do* with the text. But this isn't always the case with a writer like Plato. What Plato writes for his characters to *say* in the body of a dialogue might well be at odds with what he himself as author means to *do* with the work. The author is not his characters.

Look, no one thinks that Homer wanted to eat Hector's raw flesh, or even that he assented to the maxim, 'Strive to be the best and surpass all others.' No, we assume that Homer—as an artist, as a poet—we assume he intended to do something with and through his poetry different from what the characters say and do within it. With scholars it's

Ti esti philosophia?

altogether different. With scientists too. They intend to *do* with their texts precisely what they *say* in them.

Now think about it. In which of these two categories does Plato belong? Is he more like the artist or the scientist? This is the central element of the Platonic question. On this hinges the question of Plato's nature, on his activity and intentions *as a philosopher*.

Mary: So how do we get at Plato then, from his own point of view? If we're reading Plato primarily to learn to be philosophers in his mold, and not, as you've said before, to be disciples, scholars, or critics of Platonic doctrine, and if to learn from Plato in this way we need to get behind the doctrine to the man—how do we do that exactly? How do we get inside his head?

Professor: Yes, well, of course we can't. Not completely anyway, and not reliably. But maybe we can come close. Anyway I think it's worth a try. It's a noble risk, let's say, to borrow from the man himself. And it helps I think if we try to imagine his daily routine. How did he pass his time? Well, for sure not like Socrates. He didn't hang around the agora interrogating citizens reputed to be wise. He lived outside the city walls, in a shaded grove, in a setting most likely similar to that he depicts at the beginning of the *Phaedrus*. Remember that Plato makes Socrates *say* that he can learn only from 'men in the city,' but then he *shows* that 'rural places and the trees' in fact have much to teach him.

And considering the bulk of Plato's corpus, it's evident that he spent much of his time alone, strolling thoughtfully through his garden or in his residence writing—fully as much time, and probably more, *alone*—thinking, imagining, writing, creating—than he spent in company talking with others. Really, pick up a copy of the *Complete Works* and ask yourself when he found the time to teach, or to engage in dialectical disputations with his peers or students?

So, anyway, all this is by way of wondering what the philosophical life was to Plato, in practice. And the answer is not 'the dialogues,' or not *just* that anyway. The writings don't exhaust the life. Rather, the dialogues and—and I want to stress this—the dialogues and *all that in Plato's habits of thinking and acting led to their conception and composition*— *all* of this together is the embodiment, the literal enactment of, his conception of the philosophical life.

But enough of that. We can—we should and we will— revisit this another time. My point right now is that we shouldn't infer from Plato's founding the Academy that he was a professor in the contemporary mold, or even in Aristotle's mold. As Nietzsche observed, the dialogues are in a way the precursor to the novel. So I think it's more appropriate to think of Plato with the poets in mind, despite—or maybe even in part because of—his eagerness to draw distinctions between their activities and his own. Or, well, whether it's more *appropriate* is another matter. What I really want to say is that it's more *fruitful*, for us, I mean, fruitful with respect to our own reflections on what it is to live as a philosopher, rather than as scholars or professors of philosophy.

Christopher: And now I can't help but think of the *logos-mythos* divide.

Professor: The divide or the affinities? Philosophy *versus* poetry, or *as* poetry?

Mary: Oh, wait! Now *I'm* thinking of that essay we read on the groundlessness of belief...

Professor: Norman Malcolm, yes. Wittgenstein's friend. What about it?

Mary: Well, you know, the idea that a system or a framework, what you like to call a thought-world, supplies the boundaries within which questions, investigations, appeals to evidence and justifications take place. But the system itself is not justified by evidence. And it's not like this is a problem, a deficiency of the system. It's a conceptual requirement that our reasonings operate within the boundaries of some system. And if we want to justify these boundaries, we can manage it only by appealing to the boundary principles of some other system, which will itself then be unsupported by evidence.

Ryan: It's another version of the problem of the criterion!

Professor: Well, yes and no. Here, on Wittgenstein's or Malcolm's account, it's not a problem. The error would be in thinking of it as a problem. It's just the way reasoning works, as Mary pointed out. We appeal to a rule, for example, but we don't appeal to another rule for guidance in how to follow the rule.

Mary: Yeah, and I'm thinking this has to do with the *logos-mythos* alliance, as you called it. A philosophical system, like Platonism say, is a *mythos* which when adopted gives rise to, gives meaning and sense to, *logoi*. The system is a form of life, and forms of life don't have, or need, rational foundations. They're the *source* of rational foundations.

Tyler: And this reminds me of Quine's idea that everything that we say exists is a *posit* from a perspective *external* to the theory issuing the existential claim, but it's *real* from *within* the perspective of the theory, or the system as we're calling it.

Millie: To be is to be the value of a variable!

Tyler: Yeah, and we can never do any better than to adopt the perspective of some system at some time, even if we can't, as a matter of conceptual necessity, prove the system objectively and absolutely true.

Professor: The universe doesn't have a preferred vocabulary, as Rorty liked to say.

Christopher: And now philosophy is looking like a style of poetry. A *mythos* in which the *logoi* find their home, their meaning or significance. And the philosopher is the poet of all this.

Professor: The philosopher as a *mythologikos*, a—

Wyatt: The philosopher as a *what*?

Professor: Ha! Well, I should've known I wouldn't slip that past you, Wyatt. As a *mythologikos*, a mythologizer, let's say. That doesn't really capture it, but it'll have to do for now. We'll try to make more sense of the word next semester.

But anyway, yeah, I think what you said is right, Christopher. But to be fair, and accurate, and just to go back a minute, keep in mind that Wittgenstein tended to speak of *religion* as a form of life that's ungrounded but legitimate—if *legitimate* is the right word here—whereas he wanted to *eliminate* metaphysics, or to liberate philosophers from its bewitchments.

Ti esti philosophia?

Now, having said that, I should add that I'm not really sure why he adopted this posture. I mean, I don't understand why, on Wittgenstein's terms, one can't embrace, or, let's say, convert to, Platonism as a form of life, as you suggest, Mary. Or a Nietzschean perspective of knowing-as-creating on the far side of nihilism. Taken in the appropriate way, as an intellectual-existential framework, I don't see why one can't inhabit any thought-world one likes in a mode parallel to the religious form of life. So long as you don't imagine you're doing science. But even the scientists have to avoid this, if they're to escape Wittgenstein's censure anyway. No one's getting at objective truth here.

Wyatt: Um, alright, but wait a minute. Can we slow down and back up a bit? I'm not sure how we wound up here. I mean, if philosophy is a form of poetry, did Plato in the *Republic* intend to banish philosophers from his ideal city?

Professor: Ha! Now there's a good question, Wyatt! Bizarre and good. And good in part *because* it's bizarre. But I'm afraid we'll have to address all this next week. Now it's nearly time to go. But let me just say, before we conclude, that we now have before us pretty much all the components of a philosophical style I like to call Creative Pyrrhonism, the idea that since systems of belief are ultimately groundless, the philosopher can, and should, feel free to experiment with ideas, to create and explore new thought-worlds with a good conscience.

A *good conscience*. Right? I mean, why pretend we're in touch with the real, as if the truth itself were speaking through us, when really we're expressing our own personal subjectivity? Why not finally abandon the pose, the mask, of objectivism? Let's be honest. It's not the world. It's me. It's just me.

Anyway, the primary aim of this, admittedly idiosyncratic, application of Pyrrhonism is not *ataraxia*—though that is a goal, to be sure. Who doesn't want tranquility, or something like it, in one form or another? But anyway, no, not *ataraxia*, not ultimately anyway. The primary aim of Creative Pyrrhonism is rather a form of intellectual-spiritual liberation, philosophy as free-spiritedness. And to this end, I myself, in my own thinking life, I adopt the approach of classical Pyrrhonism, but augmented with lessons learned from Plato and Nietzsche. If nothing is true, then everything is permitted.

And by the way, just to add this closing note, if we think of Plato himself as engaged this way in the creation and exploration of a thought-world, then, as unconventional as this is to suggest, we can regard him as a Nietzschean free-spirit. More: we can think of Plato and Nietzsche together as philosophers of the future.

Wyatt: Wait! What? Plato as a free spirit? As a Nietzschean? And what do you mean, Plato and Nietzsche *together*? Now you've really lost me.

Professor: Ha! Well, that doesn't surprise me, Wyatt. We haven't discussed Nietzsche much this semester—only just in passing, like today—and we won't, either. But next semester, for those of you who'll still be around—which I think includes everyone but Ryan, Millie, and Christopher, and probably we'll have a couple of new folks too—anyway, next semester's seminar is Plato and Nietzsche. So we'll have the opportunity to go into all this in detail then.

Wyatt: So you're pairing Plato and Nietzsche in a single class? That's just so odd to me. I mean, shouldn't you call it Plato *versus* Nietzsche?

Professor: Ha! Actually, Wyatt, I did teach such a class once, and with just that title. Really. But I've changed my way of thinking since then. It's Plato *and* Nietzsche now. And, yes, as a pair. But I don't suggest they agree about everything, about *doctrine*. Of course not that. But I do contend that they agree in spirit, let's say, in philosophical style—by which I mean style of living, thinking, and writing as philosophers. Anyway, you'll see. We'll read the *Phaedo*, as I mentioned earlier. We'll read it in depth, as Nietzsche did. He taught the dialogue several times in Basel, and he liked to say that he used it to infect his students with philosophy. That may or may not have worked, I don't know. But the dialogue certainly infected him. It was on his mind throughout his active thinking life, and he wrote about it often, though usually indirectly. We'll read the relevant texts. Anyway, as I say, we'll go into all this next semester.

Wyatt: Ok, I look forward to it. But I still don't get it.

Professor: Ha! Well, alright. But that's good! That's good! We've wound up entangled in *aporia*. Lack of passage. The inability to proceed. And that's an appropriate state in which to end, no? Ha! Yes, yes, it is, for a philosophy class especially.

The creek and the cloud

Creek: Hey there, you! Who's that there, looming overhead, obstructing my view of the infinite heights and casting chill shadows on my belly? I shiver, brrr, I'm cold!

Cloud: Ah, well, and who are you to ask, and so impertinently? Who am I? Have a look. Lift your eyes. And above all don't complain. For those who know, for those who comprehend the atmospheric rule of opposites, my transient shade enhances the pleasure of a day's warmth. One must account the whole as a whole, you see, disregarding the moments as discrete units in and of themselves. Warm now; cool now: from one perspective, yes. From a narrow perspective. But stretch your limbs and broaden your view, then you'll experience the whole as refreshingly mild. Hence young humans lounging in the grass delight when I pass by. They giggle and shout and play. Be you like the children then: count not the seconds or minutes; reckon instead by afternoons.

But be all this as it may, I still wonder who you are to interrogate me so.

Creek: But can you not see for yourself? From your vantage you must mark my many meandering miles, winding through the wilds and woods, traversing the meadows along the mountain's base, catching the light and the blue sky-tones in my all-encompassing eye—except, that is, wherever I am overloomed.

Cloud: Oh my, yes—but you *are* all eye, aren't you? A single great elongated lens, a sinuous mirror, a streaming

The creek and the cloud

silver reflector. But you're a seer of unusual variety, I must say, hurrying here and tarrying there, so backward-bending, so troubled and tranquil, bright and dark, in oscillating turns. And you stare only at the sky. I must say, yours is a character provocative of wonder.

But to correct your misconception—with every good intention, I assure you—I should say, I should even insist, that I do not *loom*. Never. To loom is not my style. Linger, yes. Float, assuredly so. Drift, glide, waft—without doubt and beyond all cavil. Cousins I have who loom, to be sure, dark and aggressive and dangerous, electric flames rumbling at their hips. Towering cumulonimbus terrors all. But I myself am not like them—I am speaking now of my character, you understand—no, I am not the violent type, as I should think would be apparent to an experienced sky-gazer such as yourself. But in any case, I'm no blustery puffed-up actor, big-man of the world and all such hubbub and hurly-burly. To the contrary, I am rather a wanderer and a dreamer, mellow and contemplative, and therefore also a suitable object for others' wandering dreams.

Creek: And you're quite the talker, too, aren't you? Shifting easily, almost insensibly, from one subject to another. A skillful sophist one might suspect, if one were of a distrustful disposition. Me, I'm more inquisitive than incredulous. Thus your silky speechifying almost seduces me. Yet I am also indecisive, habitually unsettled and self-unsettling. My swirling thoughts no sooner coalesce as coherent beliefs than they blend with onrushing counter-notions, dissolve, disperse, and drift away.

Cloud: Ah, but do we not have this in common? For I too am prone to come and go, to condense and dissipate, the relevant difference between us being that my changes, my genesis and my dissolution occur as it were without warning. The phases of my becoming are all but imperceptible. How often I have overheard gawking humans on the ground express their wonder at suddenly marking my presence, then later realizing to their surprise I've altered, and later still straining their eyes but detecting only dispersing vestiges of my former self. Where have I gone? Was I ever really there? Thus some call me the visible-invisible.

Now consider yourself, are you not similar? Are you not an insubstantial substance and a dense transparency? One sees you by seeing through you.

Creek: Yes, in a sense you're correct, I admit. But I do have my moods, as you have noted. From time to time I grow dark or turbulent or both, and then I am neither reflective nor pellucid. I splash and flash with frothing foam. Or I grow viscous, thick, and immobile as molasses, on which occasions one might suspect I'm sufficiently solid to support the substance of stone. And then there are those moments I'm overshadowed by extraneous dusks and shade. I appear all gloom. As contented and even cheerful as I may be within myself, a passing stranger overhangs and darkens me. As now, for example.

Cloud: Oh, so we're back to that complaint? And here I thought we were making friends!

Creek: Friends?! Really? And can being be friends with becoming then?

The creek and the cloud

Cloud: Well, I don't see why they can't at least become friends. I refer you again to the cosmic law of opposites. But am I to understand from your remark that you conceive yourself under the category of being, as, if I may put it this way, *to on*?

Creek: Ah, oh, an intellectual! And a Hellenist no less! But anyway, yes, of course—being, or *to on*, if you prefer. Have you not yet looked me over? As I said, from your lofty perch you must comprehend the entirety of my course. Am I not here as well as there, now as well as then? Turn and look behind you. Do you not see some six miles back the little run-off falls flowing into me, constituting me, as my source and origin? And now look ahead, peer out ahead, yes, like so but farther still. Good. You see how I expand, how I mature and grow? There in the distance I am called not 'creek' but *river*. And now look you farther still beyond the remote meadows and the plains beyond them. Yes, there, yes. You observe, do you not, that I pour myself as a surge into the great sea? Now contemplate the whole, if you will, take me in in one comprehensive sweep. —And here I appeal to the principle you employed yourself in privileging afternoons as wholes over every discrete second and minute.— So, then, consider: Are not my past, present, and future simultaneously extant? Do I not both move and remain unmoving? Indeed, I do! For I am motion in repose, a self-circulating now revolving in the womb of eternity. The trickle becomes the creek; the creek becomes the river; and the river in turn becomes the sea. Yet these, my comings to be and passings away, are but temporal illusions, mere appearances. I am the whole, the extremities and the midpoint all at once. Thus in my nature I am only being, pure and ever-abiding.

Cloud: An eternal present, then? The *aei on*? Is this your self-conception? Really? Hmm. To my way of thinking, the ephemeral present is all there is. It is but a fleeting fraction, to be sure, an infinitesimal eye-blink of a moment, a mere point—nevertheless, it *is*. The past and the future on the other hand are *not*—no longer and not yet—and the cosmos is, let us say, an episodic on-going of generation and evaporation, with only the merest of threads, what we call the Now, binding the divide.

Besides, were not you yourself just recently referring to your temperamental alterations *from moment to moment* and *on occasion*, also to your constant changes of mind, the instability of your beliefs? Do you not gurgle and bend and flow? Of course you do! So, then, which is it? Are you a moving temporal multiplicity, bright here and now, gloomy there and then, or are you rather a single simultaneity?

Creek: But this is a matter of perspective, is it not? And maybe even a matter merely of a mode of speaking, a turn of phrase. In any case, I mean to say that the here-and-now is appropriate to the perspective of any particular temporal prospect—which as subjectivities we occupy necessarily—but that the temporally comprehensive conception is fully equally accurate, *sub specie aeternitatis*, as they say.

The 'I' behind my eye as manifest near my source experiences itself as coming to be, no doubt, as I experience myself expiring near the sea, and also in this moment conversing on this spot with you, I feel myself here, now. Yet, despite these spatial distinctions and temporal discontinuities, my deeper self embraces and includes all of these experiences, and even as my waters flow I myself remain, everywhere at once.

And as regards time, I'm no flunky for the A-series, no presentist, as I take you to be, restricting existence strictly to the present moment, to *this* present moment. I'm a B-series man myself, an eternalist. I admit of course that no moment other than this present moment exists *now*. But I'm quite sure that past and future moments also do exist, exist *simpliciter*, that is; tenselessly, if you will. For I cannot believe that from moment to moment the entire universe, by slipping into the past, lapses out of existence, while it bursts anew into existence with the arrival of every future moment. Just imagine the convulsions and noise of a universe uninterruptedly coming to be and passing away!

But seriously. As I understand these things, the perception of every subjectivity is temporally confined to its own present moment, but every present moment, including those called 'past' and 'future' from the perspective of every other present, must exist. My present subjectivity cannot access these other present moments, but the subjectivities that occupy them can, in fact they do, and they are doing so now—right now, during our now, other temporally confined subjectivities are perceiving their own now, which we call by the name 'past' or 'future,' precisely as they call our now 'past' or 'future' from their own perspective. So then, if you like, I will grant that the present moment alone exists, but in that case I must add that this includes, even during this present now, every past and future present moment too, each of which from its own perspective is the present now.

And what about you, my friend? You refer to yourself as *becoming*. But have you not spoken the words, 'I am'? And have you not described yourself as *this* or *that*? Indeed, you have! But if there be nothing besides becoming, then no *this* or *that* can ever really *be*, and therefore nothing *is*, including you yourself. In the fleeting fraction of your eye-blink-Now you will be no *thing* but only a vanishingly temporary locus of energy, a mere motion in a field, constructed into unity through temporary alignments and alliances of energy and force, or through external acts of cognition, or I know not how. But, in any case, you will not *be*, not, that is, as *you*.

Cloud: Ah, yes, well—but of course I never meant to suggest that I do not exist. Becoming is not nothing after all.

Creek: And I don't mean to question the 'exist' in your 'I exist.' The primary problem is rather with the 'I.' For consider: on your account, in what sense exactly is the I you take yourself to be, the I as substance, anything more than a conceptual or logical construct, an illusory pseudo-substance fabricated from insubstantial moments and infinitesimal time-points?

Cloud: Hmm, well, permit me in reply to recall an old tradition, a *palaios logos*, if you will, which distinguishes two lines of thought about the nature of reality: among the ancients one account descends from Homer, Hesiod, and Orpheus, and stretches down to Heraclitus and Empedocles, all of whom insisted that the world is a multiplicity of restless change and flow; the other account is associated

The creek and the cloud

with Xenophanes, Parmenides, and Zeno, who contended to the contrary that all is one, unchanging and eternal.

Creek: And the Hellenist reappears!

Cloud: Yes, well, be that as it may. I should like to suggest that the distinctions drawn by these opposing camps are too constricted and inflexible, as our own discussion has perhaps revealed. Might it be that being and becoming are intermingled throughout all things, and—

Creek: But wait! No, excuse me, but now you're playing the sophist again, my friend! You're deploying antilogic (I use the word in the Greek sense, you understand, as *antilogikê*) to attribute contrary properties to one and the same thing, as the ancient *antilogikoi* with their slippery sophisms made all things appear to bob up and down as on the waters of a choppy strait. But you'll not persuade me that a single self-same entity is both one and many, at rest and in motion. Besides, your proposal is biased in favor of the party of flux, is it not? For if all things are really interblended, as you suggest, then there is no fundamental unity, and hence no actual being. Is this not so?

Cloud: Ah, oh, and who's the Hellenist now—you with your talk of sophistry and *antilogikê*?! My oh my! But in any case, at least you've called me 'friend,' and that's something, I should say. But to return to the matter at hand. My present proposal is that radical flux and ephemerality characterize physical things and phenomenal objects, such as ourselves, but that there exist other entities, real beings—really real *ta onta*—to which contrary properties do not apply. If this is right, then these latter beings would be authentic unities, eternal and unchanging.

Diamythologōmen

Creek: Oh, ah! You *are* the shifty one, aren't you?! From the sophist you proceed to ape the Platonist! No wonder you're so hard to grasp! But would you really have us now confront the confounding conundrum of the one and many? An intractable enigma! Surely you don't fancy we're up to the challenge of resolving a riddle against which the boldest intellectuals have burst their brains for millennia?

Cloud: Well, but we needn't try to solve any riddles. We are only talking, after all, or thinking out loud, if you will. We're pondering at our leisure, and isn't this the superlative act of every thinking thing? No need to strive for more. Besides, we don't have the time, for I shall have to leave soon, even though the breeze today is all but non-existent.

Creek: All right, then. Very good. Well said. But since we're only talking, I trust you won't be offended if I suggest that your belief in these *ta onta*, these really real unified and unchanging beings, is an error deriving from the illusion I mentioned previously, the illusion of the I-substance, if I may call it that. For it does seem to me that you are subject to this illusion, as I infer from your tendency to speak, and presumably to think, the 'I am,' as I noted earlier. This specific misunderstanding of yourself—or, better, of your so-called 'self'—this misleads you as to the nature of reality in general.

Every subjectivity, no matter how minuscule the extent of its temporal scope, experiences itself as an effective locus and source of force, as the subject of an object's predicates, the enduring substance of which the object's qualities are transitory properties, as the active doer behind the deed—in

The creek and the cloud

short, as the reality behind the appearances. For example, you take yourself to be *the cloud*—the subject—which *is changing*—changing density or place for instance—and you imagine that you abide as substance even as your qualities come and go as accidents—at least until your every last particle of constituent matter is finally dispersed, disconnected, and dissociated; in the meantime you are—or anyway you take yourself to be—an enduring unified substance. And every subjectivity, such as yourself, casts this self-conception as an organizing template over the chaos of its sensory experience, thereby generating, literally creating, the perceptual semblance of things, the illusion of being.

But this *is* only illusory, anyway it must be according to your account. For if you really are a process of becoming, and nothing besides, then you must be deceived about who and what you are, indeed about your being anything at all. And if becoming is all there is, anywhere and anywhen, then you must also be deceived about there being anything at all beyond yourself. As I have said, if there is no being, then neither can there *be* any *this* or *that*.

Cloud: Oh, but wait! Am I to understand that you are now criticizing me for introducing being into my account of becoming? Is this really your point? I wonder, for I cannot fathom why you would object to this, you who seem to pride yourself literally on *being* being? If one of us is postulating substance here, it is you, not me.

And now quite suddenly, and much to my surprise, you speak of being as an illusion, and of substance as an error. Are you jesting with me? Do you mock me? Or is this an instance of your changing your mind, a backward flowing of your current, a bending of your course?

But wait! No, don't answer me yet. First, please, tell me this. You were speaking earlier of yourself as a single whole from falls to creek to river to sea. But what do you imagine yourself to be before the falls, or after the sea—whence come the falls, and whither goes the sea? Or does the former come into being from nothing, the latter pass away into nothingness too?

Creek: Oh, but of course I reject the insinuation that I could ever come to be from, or pass away into, non-being. But what do you have in mind exactly? Do you mean to refer to the little pools and ponds from which my falls take form, or to the rain that fills them up, and also to the water vaper into which the droplets of the sea evaporate?

Cloud: Exactly, yes! Just that! As a whole you stretch beyond the limits of falls and sea. To a coarse and imprecise sight there may appear nothing more to you than your visible components, but your being extends beyond all this, even into imperceptible meteorological processes.

Creek: Yes, I take your point and don't dispute it. Oh, yes, I am even grander than I thought! The idea pleases me!

Cloud: Indeed, and perhaps you are even grander still. Tell me: is there no stage between the water vaper and the rain? Is the cycle we've described so far complete?

Creek: Oh, ah! I see! You mean to refer to yourself, do you not? Rising water vapor condenses into clouds before raining down to infuse my stream. So my earlier conception of myself as falls-creek-river-sea accounted for only half my circular being.

The creek and the cloud

Cloud: Yes, and water vapor-cloud-rain is the other half. With that the circle is complete.

Creek: And so you, cloud, are but a phase in the circular whole that I am.

Cloud: Or *you*, creek, are but a phase in the circular whole that *I* am.

Creek: But wait! No! It can't be so, for your very being depends on my supply of water. Without me you would not exist.

Cloud: But of course I can say the same about you. For where would you be without me? Does not my rain give you life?

Creek: But in that case which of us has priority here? Which is fundamental? One of us must be more real than the other, for if I am being and you are becoming, we cannot be identical.

Cloud: But *are* you really being, and nothing besides? And *am* I really *only* becoming? I'm beginning to suspect that this cannot be right. For hasn't our discussion revealed that the matter is more complex than this? It seems that neither of us can speak of either being or becoming without introducing the contrary term. These notions are not the same, to be sure; indeed they are opposites. Yet it's as if they're somehow conjoined, so that the one inevitably accompanies the other. Thus, for example, even though you emphasize the reality of atemporal being, you admit the validity of a temporal perspective of moments of becoming, indeed of every moment of becoming as a real constituent of the great bulk of being. You are moreover tempted at times to regard all talk of being as resulting from conceptual

Diamythologōmen

misunderstandings, as an expression of illusion and error. And I, for my part, who formerly conceived of myself as a constant fluctuation of becoming—even I turn out to be composed of fleetingly brief yet actual moments of being. More, each of these moments only *appears* fleeting, from the point of view of a subjectivity confined to its particular temporal perspective, whereas actually each in itself abides eternally.

Oh, it's the generative law of opposites again! Yes, indeed, for consider this: imagine the two of us on opposite poles of a great circle, I above, you below. Imagine as well that with my left hand, which is the rain, I reach down and take your right hand, the little run-off falls, and you with your left hand, which is the sea, reach up and take my right hand, the rising drops of water vapor. Imagine us in this way forever facing one other, clasping hands, making of ourselves one great continuous circle of inter-transforming elements. Do you see? Do you envision the resulting unity in multiplicity, the rounded block of being manifest in and through the endless cycles of becoming? A mighty vision indeed!

And with this image in mind I conclude, if I may put it this way, I conclude that we are not in fact divided as mutual strangers and antagonists, but rather that we're unified as friends, brothers even, as discrete but coupled moments on the great circle of being-and-becoming.

Creek: And more than brothers, it seems to me. For if you are right, mustn't we be equally real, equally fundamental—identical even, in a sense? Is this what you mean to say?

The creek and the cloud

Cloud: Oh, ah, yes! Identical! Quite right! Even our opposition is merely apparent! And now consider the further implications. We are one, utterly identical beneath the surface of our distinct expressions. Therefore even as we speak together—disputing and agreeing in turns—even so, I am you talking to yourself, or you are me talking to myself, each of us a phase in the whole that is the other, or rather that is us. Multiple lines of a single harmony, as it were. Cloud rain creek sea cloud rain creek, and so on and on unendingly, an eternally recurring cycle, a circle of elements revolving so rapidly as to appear, to become, as actually to be, motionless. Yes, this now strikes me as the nature of being, a tightly bound circuit of becoming.

Creek: Oh, ah, yes! I see the vision too, and a profound sight it is! It's as though in the course of our discussion we've plumbed the depths to resurface bearing a fact from the foundations of the world.

Cloud: Yes, a fine formulation, that. Though I myself prefer to regard our vision as sublime. For as I see it, we've attained a height of thought that shines with the brightness of a sun. I see illumination where you, apparently, see dark obscurity.

Creek: No, not obscurity. Rather fundamentality, the grounds of things. I observe the uncovering of what was covered, the lifting of veils. For mustn't one dive deep in order to mount the summit of truth? And hasn't it always been the boldest exploratory thought-divers who've introduced us to our peak experiences and insights?

Cloud: Or the solitary star-sages who've carried their flames from their mountains to our valleys? Hence the ancients originally erected their altars on the crests of the highest hills, the better to converse with their heroes and their sky-gods.

Creek: Or in caves beside their rivers, sacred to chthonic deities, passageways to the underworld.

—Oh, but here we are disagreeing again, entangled in opposition!

Cloud: But surely we have learned by now that opposition generates unity—or, rather, that opposition is but the mask behind which unity often hides. I have called opposition generative, but now it seems to me that this is a misconception resulting from our limited, and limiting, perspective. Opposition appears to generate unity only because the manifest opposites are visible poles on a continuum which in itself is anteriorly unified. He who fails initially to detect the unity, seeing nothing besides the opposites, will, on finally perceiving unity, take it to have come to be. But really it existed all along, unnoticed.

Creek: Yes, good. I like that. And somehow now I am thinking of high mountain caves, portals to the depths whose entrance is on the heights. Also of mountains in the sea, some of which are very tall indeed, though totally submerged. Thus one might say that to plumb our depths we must mount our highest heights, and to ascend our heights we must descend into our deepest depths. One might even say that every self-reflective thinking thing is both a pinnacle abyss and an abyssal summit.

Cloud: It's the unity of opposites again! Or rather the unmasking of unity behind the veil of apparent opposition, to employ your analogy.

The creek and the cloud

Creek: Yes, or, wait—what's that? I didn't quite make out what you said. Speak up. I believe you referred to opposition as a mask concealing original unity. Is that right?

Cloud: Yes, friend, you heard me correctly. But, oh, I'm afraid I can't speak up, for I am dissipating. As much as I hate to conclude our conversation, I must withdraw. But I did mention earlier that I should soon depart.

Creek: Ah, yes, indeed you did. I recall it. Shall we therefore review the results of our conversation, before our time together expires?

Cloud: Yes, let's.

Creek: But have we reached any stable conclusions? For it seems to me that we have each abandoned our original totalizing point-of-view to adopt and incorporate something of the other's way of thinking.

Cloud: Yes... I, I do believe you're right about that... Moreover, I...

Creek: Ah, friend! I cannot hear you! Your voice is fading fast. Shall I continue on my own? And perhaps you can indicate assent or disagreement in some manner other than speaking? Yes? No? Ah, I don't know, I can't tell; but I'll take that for a 'yes.'

Cloud: Yes... Please, do contin—

Creek: I shall try to go on, my friend. Thus: The eternal and the temporal; unity and multiplicity; being and becoming. Each member of these pairs of putative opposites is real, as fully as actual as the other. They are partners in equal standing in the construction of the cosmos. More, they aren't even really opposites. For eternity is the infinite collection of temporal moments, each of which in itself

Diamythologōmen

abides eternally. The one as a whole is constituted by the multiplicity of its parts bound together, and each of these parts is itself a unity. And being, too—yes, even being is but the unvarying repose of the multiple phases of becoming gathered together unto themselves.

Thus it is as you have said, friend cloud, that whoever speaks of one member of these pairs inevitably invokes the other. To affirm a whole one must affirm each of its parts. By affirming any present now one affirms simultaneously the past moments that brought it forth, and the future moments which it must bring forth in its turn. There is no saying Yes to the one without thereby affirming the many, no affirming the discrete moments of becoming without saying Yes to the continuum of being.

What do you say, my friend? Do you approve this formulation?

Cloud: ...

Creek: Ah, but your silence does unsettle me! I lose my confidence, doubt myself. Perhaps I have misconceived these matters. For now it occurs to me that reality—to which I have just referred as a cosmos—might be instead an indeterminate, indefinable, and uncategorizable chaos, having no definite structure in and of itself. Objectively perspectival, if I may employ a paradoxical expression.

Cloud: ...

Creek: Or, maybe, given the conditions of our subjectivity, we can have no knowledge of the nature of reality, including whether it is objectively anything, or any way, at all, which is to say whether it even has, or is, a nature, as chaos or as cosmos.

The creek and the cloud

Cloud: ...

Creek: Ah, but as I say, your silence unsettles and stresses me! And... and, well, I don't know. Perhaps there is more to these matters than I have understood, yet another option, a conception less ambiguous, and thereby more appealing to the heart and mind. But I cannot think my way to it, not without your assistance, friend. But are you there? Won't you add a final word to our discussion, just one concluding note of resolution? Please!

...

Philia and *sophia*

Six weeks seems almost a season. Might as well be. Bare branches brown lawns and log-fire smoke. It's December yet, this side of perihelion, but low grey clouds and cold these afternoons. Snow by sunset, maybe before I'm home. Unusual for Nashville, December snow. I remember thirty years ago, top down and comfortable Christmas day. Cool nights but… God was still alive then, if indistinct… though nebulous… if indistinct.

Stop! I'm walking not to write but to think. Τί ἐστι φιλοσοφία? Wander but don't revise. *Ti esti philosophia?* And enough already with the *Symposium*'s account of philosophy as the search for knowledge! Unmediated knowledge of the Forms, the really real, *ta onta*. The love of wisdom: love as lacking, desiring, seeking; wisdom as knowledge of the truth. Purported account. The standard reading. A petrified exegesis. By now it's just so boring, and anyway incorrect, or plausible only within the frame of the dialogue, and even then from only one exchange.

This is central to the book. For the philosopher of the future 'knowing' is *creating*. The classroom chapter only just begins to address this. I could've gone on, but it would be too long. I'll include at least two more each of the thinking and classroom chapters, elaborate the theme there.

See the trees, stark grey ghosts towering, shadowing overshadowing the hedge-rowed streets of a bourgeois neighborhood, the manicured lawns and tidy back yards. Battened down for ice today. Andy says he prefers to walk the alleyways, feels more like Europe. I don't mind it myself. Not that I crave the material comforts and security of the bourgeoisie, but I don't mind living among those who do. (Yes, well, maybe I do too.) Everyone can't be a bohemian artist—and shouldn't be. No demimonde if the whole round *monde* is peopled by antinomians. Besides, most around here are bobos, liberals in their paradise.

So-called liberals. Neoliberals. Whole food health food hungry for wealth and status. Status and wealth.

Who then is the philistine, the man who drinks box wine, or the man who fancies that savoring wine is a mark of high culture?

But the houses and trees are pleasant enough. And the sidewalks are convenient. All in all a soothing aesthetic. Doesn't begin to approach the sublime (Sils-Maria), but there's beauty, or at least tranquility. In the natural element anyway.

And the sanity-inducing stone.

But back to the book. Anyway art and mass culture are each better off when separated, in opposition even. The *necessity* of an underground is essential, resistance to the eccentric, and even a measure of antagonism. The struggle inspires and fortifies. The Beats—the Beats are not my favorites—the Beats came of age as artists in the repressive fifties, young men sporting khakis, sweaters, and crew cuts. By the end of the sixties they were spent—sloppy, fat, drunk. The liberated sixties, sire of the greasy seventies.

The initial stages of decadence smell sweet. Later, when the whole society decomposes, everything just stinks.

Diamythologōmen

Sils-Maria and the sanity-inducing stone. *La casa Muccini sul Conca*. Summer still six months away; last summer like it never happened, a half-remembered dream. I no longer *feel* it.

And—it's Thursday, so seven, six, thirteen, thirteen days till classes start. The Plato-Nietzsche seminar should be good. As for the rest, the bureaucratic busy-work, assessment and administrative bloat—early retirement, early retirement, early retirement. The humanist's refrain these days.

But back to the book. *Ti esti philosophia*? Why not philosophy as Socrates at the beginning of the *Symposium*, loitering on the porch, lost in thought, having 'turned his *nous* toward himself'? An instance of the same strange act Alcibiades recounts at the dialogue's end. Socrates standing out all night reflecting, pondering, inquiring—*sunnoein, skopein, zētein*, I believe these are the words—motionless through to dawn. Warrior-philosopher exploring the labyrinth of his mind.

The truth is in the deep. Or anyway something's lurking down there, hiding out. Sounds like snorts and stomping hooves. Too dark to see.

Nietzsche and his Zarathustra Stone.

Or the love of wisdom as the 'madness and Dionysian frenzy of the philosopher'? Plato's insight delivered through the persona of a drunken profligate. *Al·ki·bi·a·dês*, the mask. Eleusinian priest. Bull god. The Minotaur. Brilliant but self-destructive, tyrannically erotic.

The philosopher's love of beauty in the *Phaedrus* is a madness granted by the gods, a gift of radical eccentricity,

Philia and sophia

untimeliness. It's not the prosaic search for knowledge, though it does *make use* of knowledge. The philosopher is a knower, but more than that inspired, possessed, mad.

Philosophy then as Plato's activity of conceiving and composing the dialogues. *Theia mania, pankalê paidia*. Divine madness, comprehensively exalted play. Plato as the madly creative pondering man. Plato as the frenzied—

Ach! Stop writing! It's so hard *just to think* when you intend to include the thoughts in the book. Instead you tend to *think for the book*. But thinking for the book isn't thinking. It's writing. What you want is really to think, and later to record the thoughts. Revise, edit, and elaborate when writing it down, and again when later reviewing it. Fine. But the general content, the framework and thematics, the images structure flow and movement should come from authentic thinking. It's a devious procedure.

And then of course you're entangled in a meta-thinking. The self-reflective spiral. As now. Thinking about the book instead of thinking. And thinking about thinking about the book instead of thinking. And thinking about thinking about the book instead of thinking instead of thinking. And again you're out of your head.

God, I bet the neighbors love the sight of that 'For Sale' sign. The lawn's always such an overgrown mess.

Alright dammit, stop already! Just stop. ... Now ease back in. Sink down. Warm water. ... Good, quiet now, relax. Consider the trees' fractal branches. Let it blur. Forget yourself. Just walk.

...

Diamythologōmen

And why assume that any single character expresses or embodies Plato's conception of philosophy? The dialogue *as a whole* is an expression of his idea—and not just all the characters taken together, nor even including the dramatic framing. Rather the *fact* of the dialogue, as artifact, as a work of art. Unveils him as—what did Plato intend to do when he sat down to write? (cover and uncover) Nothing like a professor intends today. *Professional* philosopher. APA. PhilPapers. Citation count. Look closer than even between the lines. Press behind the words, behind the page.

I don't want to learn from Diotima. Not even as a mystic initiation. And not from Socrates either. I want to learn from Plato, apprentice to the master thinker-artist. Even if he's hidden behind his words, only indirectly on display, and therefore difficult to identify. Even so. One has to gaze penetratingly through the dialogue, as through a translucent but elaborately ornamented sphere... as through an elaborately ornamented but still translucent sphere, to discover the mind of the man who produced it. This is the mind I want to know. Not the text, but the hand that composed the text. The creative intellect that guided the hand. The—

"Oh damn!" ... Goddamned dog! Scares me every time. "*Cattivo!*" Glad he wasn't loose when we walked by this morning. Scialla would've thrown a fit. Goddamn dog!

Cerberus, and... And the cave-bear hermit of Sils-Maria, standing beside the stone. What's *he* thinking? Now, I mean. Right now. Which is then, now, but now, then.

Anyway, the *Symposium*'s just one dialogue, and Plato's art—philosophical art—is manifest in the total collection of his works. And still there's more to the man than he put into his writings. More to the man *as a philosopher*. One wants to observe him in action, moving through his day. One wants to talk to him, and not about the dialogues. Or anyway not as a scholar would speak with him. Not about doctrine. Rather about himself, the instincts and habits of his thinking life. How did he generate ideas? Did he conjure them in dreams, awaken with novel thoughts in his morning mind's embrace? How and with what intention did he structure or plot his works? Did he surprise himself, his intellectual-creative choices? How did he pass his afternoons, his evenings under the wheeling stars? Beneath what trees did he walk ('the rural places and the trees') along which paths? Beside which stone did *he* stand?

Stop staring at the sidewalk! Your shoes! Look up at the trees, see the sky. The atmospherics facilitate thought. And don't just think—*feel*. Breathe it in, the afternoon. What there is of nature around and between the houses. The coming snow. Sils-Maria and the sanity-inducing stone. Inhale. *Think!*

But relax. Just let it come.

Beauty and insight. The beauty of insight. The broad magnolias interspersed among the naked scratching limbs contribute more than color. Mood. See. So tall, so old, so 'Confederate grey and magnolia green.' Robin Hill Road. It's a pleasant view, it's evocative, looking down this rolling street. The sky. Still, I *am* eager for the snow, the 'colorless all-color of atheism.'

Nostalgic chill. The evening hush. Snow-swirl in the diffuse illumination of a streetlight, drifting at angles in the wind. The light touch on the tongue, a fairy's finger. Icy afternoons, hearth and fire and quilt. Snow day home from school. From work. Early morning abed.

The whiteness of the whale.

The womb.

And Melville looked out on his snowy fields as through a port-hole on the sea.

Art and madness.

Snow-swirl.

Art and madness.

Wistfulness.

Art and madness.

Pondering man.

Infinity-wistfulness...

...

Give the spirit dangerous freedom. Knowing is *creating*...

...

Is truth discovered by my intellect or created by my imagination and posited by will?

Truth is out there in the world, *as* the world, as reality, which intellect discovers and understands, to which the will then assents. Truth is primary, will subordinate.

Or imagination generates, and will postulates, a thought-world, which intellect then rationalizes, and thereby it becomes the truth, the world, reality. Imagination and will are primary, truth subordinate.

...

'The One is the many,' Nietzsche says Heraclitus says. But if the One is a multiplicity, how then is it a one? If the One is the totality of the buzzing hive of multiple subjectivities subjectively regarded as a unity—the One, as one, really just is multiplicity.

Which implies that there is no One.

Let's say then that the One really is a unity. In that case, how and why and when does it become a multiplicity?

From eternity?

But this too implies there is no One.

Let's say the One is a unity that knows itself in, through, and as, multiplicity.

But if the One is self-reflective, it's already divided from itself, within itself. And therefore, yet again, it's not a unity but a multiplicity.

And if this world of multiplicity, including multiple subjectivities, is an objectification of the self-reflectivity of the One, is the One aware of this? Does it know it's creating the world, or does it believe it has discovered it?

Let's say the One suspects that its subjectivity generates the world, that reality is an objectification of its self-perception and -contemplation, even of its self-knowledge. Then being the self-reflective type it must wonder whether it really knows itself, whether it might not misunderstand itself. And thus the One will think its way into various puzzles and skeptical disturbances. It must worry whether the world is dependent but distinct, as the pot to the potter, or dependent and indistinct, as the thought to the thinker or the dream to the dreamer.

And if the One concludes that the world exists within and as a mode of its subjectivity, it must wonder whether the world reflects its essence accurately or diverges as an artifact of its creative imagination. More, it must wonder whether it generates the world but not intentionally, or not completely freely, whether its will commands its creative act. The world might be an involuntary expression of the One's subconscious depths.

And if the One is dreaming the world into being, then it's dreaming. And if it's dreaming then it doesn't know itself, therefore the world most likely isn't an accurate reflection of its essence. More, if it's dreaming it can't be certain its reasoning about what it is and what it's doing is sound. Even including *that* reasoning.

The One then as a skeptical philosopher, as aporetic, confused, as turning around into itself. Against itself. Self-engulfing.

Or maybe there's no single subject thinking anything at all, neither I nor the world nor the One. Maybe there's no unified focal-source of all this subjective activity, there's only source-less subjectivity, only subjective becoming.

...

Maybe the world is me thinking myself, the ontological objectification of my self-contemplation.

Or I am the objectification of the world, or of some subjectivity therein, thinking itself.

Or I and the world, everything together as a whole, is the objectification of some x thinking itself.

Imagine this x as the One. And now imagine the One wondering:

'Maybe the world is me thinking myself, the ontological objectification of my self-contemplation.

'Or I am the objectification of the world, or of some subjectivity therein, thinking itself.

Philia and *sophia*

'Or I and the world, everything together as a whole, is the objectification of some x thinking itself.

'Imagine this x as the One. And now imagine the One wondering:'

"Maybe the world is me thinking myself, the ontological objectification of my self-contemplation.

"Or..."

And so on and on unendingly, an infinite series of postulated Ones postulating Ones.

In that case, I myself am one of these Ones. I imagined myself as originator of these thoughts, postulating a One postulating a One, and so on and on unendingly. But if there's an infinite series of postulated Ones postulating Ones, and so on and on unendingly, then I'm not the originary thinker of the thought. I'm one among the infinite series of Ones, postulated by a prior One, postulating a posterior One.

So I am a One myself, which is to say I am the One. I. Am the One. It's the simplest hypothesis.

Or simpler still that all this is the thinking of no thinker—source-less subjectivity. There is no One.

In that case, am I the One thinking itself out of being? The One as active intellectual nihilist, even including itself, which is to say myself, which is to say— ...

The mad One, lost in the mirror of its mind. The *regressus ad infinitum*.

Wait, what?! Where was I?

Oh, a flake!

Was it? Where?

There!

Diamythologōmen

Where? I don't see it.

The fantasies of a philosopher are more precious than the collected works of a scholar's pedantry. (Here, I was here.) Nietzsche and Wilamowitz, for example. *Wissenschaft* or *die fröhliche Wissenschaft*. Later in life, did the old man regret it? The petty cavils and criticisms. Did he ever finally understand?

Ti esti philosophia?

Yes, precisely here.

Yes, there, a flake! And another one too!

Evidently philosophy is bound up with wisdom, *sophia* as its *telos*, but what exactly is *sophia*, and who is the sage?

Solon as usual comes first to mind. Law-giver and poet, man of experience and 'I grow old always learning many things.'

But Heraclitus says that much learning doesn't make one wise. 'I searched myself,' he says. Master of the *ricerca interiore*, thought-diver, underwater cartographer of the mind.

And what did he find?

So deep is the *logos* of the soul, its limits are undiscoverable.

Several now—and here it comes!

Nietzsche maintains the phenomenality of the inner world, too. So is wisdom straight or crooked, then, the sublime or the profound?

You're asking me? I'm just trying to think, and to enjoy the season's first snow. *Nevica!*

Philia and *sophia*

(Evidently) So I said, but maybe there's no such state as wisdom, no such type as the sage. Maybe these are only words. And maybe the philosopher has no *telos*.

Or, or maybe there's a sense in which the philosopher is the higher type.

Plato and Nietzsche.

Oh, wait—yeah, *maybe the philosopher is superior to the sage*.

Ok, yeah, of course! Now work that out.

Our words mislead us—*philosophos*—etymological misdirection. The type we call a sage is *not* the type the philosopher seeks to be. To become. Solon for example. No, the philosopher doesn't seek to be any type other than he is. Right?

Right. If the philosopher as a type were seeking x (*sophia*), then upon attaining x would he become a different type, or operate in a different mode? But which different type or mode? Certainly not the sage-type, or sage-state. Think about it. Plato didn't aim to become a Solon, or to trade composing dialogues for meditating and sermonizing like the Buddha. No, I can't imagine Plato, or Nietzsche, as any other than as they were, certainly not as a higher type. There is no higher type.

The sage is not the butterfly to the philosopher's caterpillar, the oak tree to his acorn.

Right, that's good. So don't identify the *philosophos* by assuming he seeks to be a sage. Don't mistake *philia* and *sophia* for *seeking* and *sage-state*.

Exactly!

Diamythologōmen

In the case of the philosopher, then, take *philia* for what it is, friendship. And *sophia*—well, that's trickier, but thinking—yeah, playful thinking, creative intellectuality.

So the *philosophos* is, let's say, a friend of thinking. A *friend of thinking*—right! And what do friends do together? They keep company, and they talk and laugh and dream and play.

Ok, yeah, that's good. Conceive the type philosopher, not with the sage-state in mind as *telos*, but regarding Plato and Nietzsche as exemplars of the type. They didn't seek to be any different than they were, to transcend philosophy into wisdom. As philosophers they were already the higher type.

So here's my error, which maybe I've just corrected. I've addressed *ti esti philosophia?* by analyzing the noun into *philos* and *sophia*, which is good—if obvious—and I abandoned the idea that the *philos* in this context is a seeker, also good—and not so obvious—but I've tried to understand *sophia* with reference to the sage-type. The philosopher as aiming for the sage-state. Yeah, and here's where I've gone wrong—in the *Moby-Dick* and *Plato and Nietzsche* books, and even just a minute ago.

So, let's say that there *is* such a type as the sage—Solon, for example. Fine. But the *sophia* of the sage is not the philosopher's *sophia*.

And the philosopher *does* have a *telos*, but it's not attainment of the sage-state. It's rather the ongoing activity of philosophy. The continuous play of the friend of thinking.

Sorry, Diotima, but *this* is the good the philosopher desires to possess forever.

So, despite what I've been thinking for some time, *the philosopher and the sage are distinct types*. They're related, of course, they're similar in a sense, say considered together in contrast to the athlete or the craftsman. But they're definitely distinct, and between the two the philosopher is the higher type.

Yes, all right, this is key. So long as I conceived *sophia* as a state on a continuum with *philosophia* but beyond it, which the philosopher lacks and seeks to attain, the *sophos* appeared superior to the *philosophos*, as actual to potential. Solon superior to Plato. But this is all wrong. The two types are distinct, and *the philosopher is the higher type*.

The friend of thinking. Yeah, and this is better I think than 'thinker-artist.' Less immediately explicit as to content, but more euphonious.

Oh, ok, it's really coming down now. Wow! I didn't even notice. I've been thinking, just thinking, and a steady line of thought too. Sustained. And now I'm almost home. Not once with the book in mind. Not once. And no self-reflective loops or meta-doubts, only the flow of ideas, *as the flow*, *as* the thinking, and nothing besides. *Sum, ergo cogito*. Ha! The thinking life, the ideal—and even better if I can remember it.

So: the philosopher's superior to the sage. Remember that. The friend of thinking. Write that down. Plato's no potential Solon, Solon's not a Plato actualized, butterfly to his caterpillar. Right. Remember that. Butterfly to his caterpillar. The *philosophos* as the higher type. Write it down.

Diamythologōmen

All right. Almost there. The higher type. Remember that. The philosopher's superior to the sage. Write it down. The friend of thinking. Inside. *Philia* and *sophia*. Write it all down.

"Eccomi, Scialla! Sono a casa! Sì, ciao, ciao! Brava! Brava, Sciallina! Hai visto fuori? Hai visto? Vieni qua. Look outside! See—it's snowing! Nevica, nevica, *nevica!*"

Regressus ad infinitum

I: Hello.

Mirrorme: Oh my! Hello, you.

I: Hello. How are you?

Mirrorme: I'm well, thank you—especially now that I see you.

I: After all this time.

Mirrorme: Too much time. Yes. It's been far too long. And you? How are you?

I: I'm well too, thank you.

Mirrorme: And are you comfortable?

I: I am, yes. I am. In this chair.

Mirrorme: Same chair, different house.

I: Different life.

Mirrorme: And in this life, are you comfortable?

I: …

Mirrorme: Anyway it's good to see you. It's been years since last we met.

I: Since last we spoke.

Mirrorme: I've missed you. I've grown old missing you.

I: I've grown old myself. See. And what about our youth?

Mirrorme: What about our youth?

I: Yesterday I read a book which began with a man awakening from a disturbing dream, of himself as a child walking with his father. He arose from bed trembling, almost weeping from the stress of unresolved anxiety. I thought to myself how strange it is that a grown man suffers so from the events and emotions of even his earliest childhood.

Mirrorme: They say you can't go home again. I suspect you can never leave.

I: Yes, it's as though the psyche were a thin membrane, resilient but extraordinarily thin; it undulates as beneath it churns a tempest of sorrow, rage, and fear. Confusion. Chaos.

Mirrorme: Also exuberance, joy, good will, and cheerfulness.

I: Also these, of course. But—

Mirrorme: Inevitably there is the *but*.

I: We expend such energy against the storm, straining to contain it, to keep the squalls in check and cordoned off from our daily conscious state. Our attitudes and moods.

Mirrorme: Most of this unconsciously.

I: The psychic underground. But—

Mirrorme: But?

I: At times the slightest chance occurrence—a scent, a lightning-flash of memory, a melody or lyric—and the tornadic gloom revolves into the light.

Mirrorme: Into the light, yes. Of awareness.

I: And it manifests in various ways. For example—and here I indulge a naive romantic fantasy, I know. But I'm self-critical enough to realize this—

Mirrorme: —and sufficiently self-reflective—

I: —to acknowledge that, even so, it's persistent and sincere. Therefore I take it seriously.

Mirrorme: As you should.

I: Should I? Sometimes I wonder.

Regressus ad infinitum

Mirrorme: ...

I: In any case, from time to time I ache to burn it all down. My life. From rage or frustration or despair, sometimes even from ecstatic high-spiritedness. To abandon everything, to leap into the tempest distantly deposited—elsewhere, else-when—set down to live as a hermit or a contemporary Cynic. Heraclitus in his temenos, Nietzsche among his reflective mountains' eyes.

Mirrorme: And the radical version of this fantasy?

I: The psyche's membrane ruptured at last—irreparably entattered.

Mirrorme: What you want is madness.

I: A final psychic break.

Mirrorme: And how do you envision this manifesting?

I: Well, of course I understand about the institutionalized insane, strangers to themselves, their eyes trained on invisible horizons—I understand they're not exploring intellectually, or psychically-spiritually, mapping numinous beyond-worlds and alternate planes of reality, blissfully communing with sublime phenomena. Of course I understand this.

Mirrorme: Do you?

I: I believe I do.

Mirrorme: Very well. Let's say you do. So?

I: Therefore maybe it isn't actual madness that attracts me. Perhaps rather the fancy of madness is hyperbole, a brief but recurring hypertrophy of the impulse to leave it all behind, to remove to another place, a naive time and place, more natural, to live alone in a tree trunk or a cave, as an artist-hermit.

Diamythologōmen

Mirrorme: A thinker-artist hermit, yes. But actual madness too. It's irrational but real; it's in you. For ask yourself: Is the madness an exaggerated wanderlust, or is the drive to disappear a symptom of latent madness, a concentrated manifestation, a particularized eruption?

I: But—

Mirrorme: Inevitably there is the *but*. But consider the commonalities in the events, experiences, or ideations that disrupt the functioning of your psyche.

I: When you've finally had your fill of everything, you suspect there was nothing to be had to begin with. Buying, wearing, eating, drinking, smoking, seeing, fucking something new won't change that.

Mirrorme: Yes, well, there's no need to be crude.

I: Pardon me, but—after all, we're alone here, are we not? And I do mean to indicate degraded and degrading acts. Circumlocutions and euphemisms would be misleading, and in this case disingenuous.

Mirrorme: Yes, very well then. Go on.

I: Last summer in Europe it struck me that a city is just a city, even a city as beautiful or significant as Paris, Florence, or Athens. One must visit once, to be sure. Twice or three times even. But eventually one wears out its wonders.

Mirrorme: One has seen the *David* so many times.

I: And the Parthenon.

Mirrorme: One acknowledges the craftsmanship.

I: As one must. It's undeniable.

Mirrorme: But the beauty drains away.

I: From the work, or from one's spirit.

Mirrorme: And which of these two is it, do you think?

Regressus ad infinitum

I: I fear it's the latter.

Mirrorme: And I'm afraid the former is more fearful still.

I: Really?

Mirrorme: Yes.

I: So, if there's no beauty in this world—

Mirrorme: Nor ugliness.

I: If reality is aesthetically neutral—you say this is worse than if it's rich with objective content but the subject can't experience it?

Mirrorme: In the latter case one could at least imagine that one's previous spells of beauty were veridical, and one could hope to have such encounters again. One could even strive toward that end with realistic expectations of success. A man can heal himself after all.

I: Maybe. Maybe not.

Mirrorme: Maybe not, quite right. But in any case, one definitely cannot change the world, not in this regard anyway—introducing objective beauty where none really exists. One isn't God, the singular source and focus of the true, the good, and the beautiful.

I: The problem is that life intervenes—the crassness and trivialities of this modern workaday world intervene between reality and one's spirit.

Mirrorme: Or one's spirit itself is corrupted by modernity.

I: Infected as with a virus.

Mirrorme: The disease of disillusionment.

I: Disenchantment.

Diamythologōmen

Mirrorme: But tell me. Do you imagine there's something different over here?

I: Over there? In there with you? No. But somewhere. I believe its secret name is 'Else.'

Mirrorme: And if this somewhere else is nowhere, neither manifest nor occult?

I: It's this that I'm afraid of.

Mirrorme: Then you're afraid of the real.

I: Of what might be real, yes. I admit it.

Mirrorme: Of walking the path of endless aimlessness.

I: Some say the natural world alone is endlessly abundant and rewarding.

Mirrorme: And maybe not even that.

I: Probably not even that. In any case, what I mean to say is that the real is not enough. I'm dissatisfied with the possibilities on offer in this world.

Mirrorme: The real is not enough. I understand.

I: Do you?

Mirrorme: I believe I do. You fear the real and long for something else.

I: Yes.

Mirrorme: And this something else, being different from the real, can only be the unreal.

I: Yes, maybe, and?

Mirrorme: Well, there's a name for the desire for that which is not.

I: There is?

Mirrorme: Yes, nihilism.

I: No—

Mirrorme: No? There's no such name?

I: There's such a name, of course. But I reject it. It doesn't apply to my condition.

Mirrorme: Doesn't it?

I: No. I don't deny this world, neither do I suffer from it, not regularly anyway.

Mirrorme: But you have your moods.

I: I have my moods, I do. But don't we all? Besides, it's not meaning or purpose or truth I'm after, but existential and intellectual freedom, creative expansion and ascent. Not to worship at the throne of something greater, but to be that something greater for myself. Or anyway something different, something new. To experience, imagine, think, and feel something beyond the ordinary. Otherwise eventually it's all just so banal.

Mirrorme: For a certain type of spirit.

I: Yes, and I'm reminded now of this from Nietzsche's notes: 'Profound aversion to reposing once and for all in any one total view of the world. Fascination of the opposing point of view—

Mirrorme: 'Refusal to be deprived of the stimulus of the enigmatic.'

I: Exactly! Yes, exactly that!

Mirrorme: I see. And now, considering all this together with your creative-intellectual drive, it strikes me less as nihilism than a variety of Romanticism.

I: Yes, well, I do confess to certain Romantic tendencies.

Mirrorme: Of the overflowing and gift-giving type? Or of the needful and despairing type? Speaking of Nietzsche. The question is whether you suffer from a superabundance or an impoverishment of life. This distinction makes all the difference in the world.

I: Yes, I can see that it would. And although I admit to occasionally descending into troughs of despair—I've noted the fact already myself—still, I like to believe that my deeper and more persistent motivations are akin to fullness and the joy of bestowing. I am active after all, in my intellect and imagination, and creative rather than destructive. Indeed, one might regard my bouts of pain as symptoms of spiritual pregnancy, for I transform my thoughts and moods into expressions of the arts of living and philosophy. I aim to anyway.

Mirrorme: But still there is the aching.

I: Yes, and pain is never good in itself, even if one affirms the whole of which it is a part.

Mirrorme: Yes, you're right. And now I'll revise my diagnosis yet again. What ails you I think is a strain of infinity-wistfulness.

I: Infinity-wistfulness?

Mirrorme: A melancholy yearning to transcend the limits of the merely human. For some this manifests as a drive to conquer or establish empires. For others as art or engineering on a grand scale. For the more self-reflective and skeptical types as a perpetual wandering, sometimes geographically, but more often psychologically, intellectually and spiritually.

I: Yes! To break the bonds of one's mind. The bondage that is the mind.

Mirrorme: One feels trapped, hemmed in, frustratingly confined by the physical, emotional, and cognitive limitations of the human organism, of the bounded intellect and imagination in particular. One longs for radical transgression, release and liberation.

I: To shatter the self and disperse among the elements. To finally disappear.

Mirrorme: But not by way of annihilation.

I: No, it's not death I'm after—

Mirrorme: Not at all.

I: But expansion and absorption. To embrace and be embraced by the whole; to suffuse and be suffused; to integrate; to be everywhere and nowhere at once. In short, to leave myself behind.

Mirrorme: You know, the way you speak you remind me of—

I: Yes, I know. I sense it too.

Mirrorme: Tell the story then.

I: ...

Mirrorme: Please. It's been so long. Besides, there's insight there into what we're trying to describe.

I: Very well. Ok, so. My earliest memory is of a dream, but I don't recollect it as a dream, rather as a vision. It involves a creek, another world—within, below, or behind this world—and a cloud.

Mirrorme: Yes, yes—the creek and the cloud!

I: The creek and the cloud, indeed. But to be begin. At eight years old I experienced passage through a gateway to another universe—as in time I came to conceive the event—while playing on the bank of a creek that ran through the fields along the edge of town. The water cascaded through a sinuous channel streaming down from the hills to the north, rushing over stones and broken branches, splashing and catching the light. In the mossy borderland between the fields and the woods beyond, the creek bed expanded to form an oblong basin, where the current slowed and the water settled into a small translucent pool. Murmuring undulations flowed in arcing circuits as the tide rushed in against the standing water, then decelerated and rocked against the banks. On the farther end the water spilled out through a narrow decline, at which point it hurried on its way to the river.

Dragonflies skittered along the surface of this pool, while, beneath their tiny tarsi, tadpoles and true minnows swam among the reeds and water-grasses, which swayed with the current as in a breeze. The minnows' darting feedings from the surface set concentric circles expanding across the water, which reflected light on the sandy bed below, all sun-dappled and fluctuating. And the otherworldly and strangely plaintive croaking of the creek-frog suffused the atmosphere with an air of melancholy mystery.

As a child I loitered afternoons on the inclined bank beside this pool, tossing leaves into the water for makeshift travel-boats, dreaming of exotic destinations, chief among them the mystic realm beneath the ripples so different from my own. Silent, warm, idyllic. I fantasized that if I were smaller I could enter the place and experience directly a cosmos of astonishing beings and novel ways of life. I longed to make it so.

Mirrorme: And did you? Did you ever?

I: Yes, well, you know as well as I do.

Mirrorme: Yes, well, of course I do. But still...

Regressus ad infinitum

I: But still. All right, so. One day while playing as usual beside the pool, barefoot in the sun, I reached out for a tadpole, a jar in my left hand, and I fell into the water. Yet I was not afraid, for I could tell it was meant to be. I relaxed and allowed myself to sink, and to contract. Then, fully submerged, I swam through the depths delightedly, no bigger than a tadpole myself. I inhabited a sort of wonderland which I explored and charted with my mind, the fantastical cartographer.

Mirrorme: The fantastical cartographer!

I: On one of my circuits around the near side of the pool, a notch in the sloping bank just below the surface of the water caught my eye.

Mirrorme: It beckoned you.

I: It beckoned me, yes. Inside I discovered an illuminated grotto of dancing air, shimmering light, and colored walls flowing like mercury. A warm parlor radiant with the scent of spring flowers. In the center reclined—or sat, or stood, or all these postures at once—a striking, sensuous woman, a species of genie-enchantress. Her dark hair streamed about her shoulders as if it were of water or of wind, and she held her arms outstretched, her diaphanous pink gown billowing. I'd known this woman for millennia, I understood, but I could not speak her name. Therefore I approached in silence. When I stood before her she took my head between her hands, pulled my face to hers and stared into my eyes. I saw myself a figure in her pupils, but not as myself. I appeared an altogether different sort of being, the world around me unrecognizable.

Mirrorme: Unfathomable.

Diamythologōmen

I: I flushed then with a paradoxical sentiment of thrilled tranquility, and in that moment I touched eternity—or so I apprehend it now; at the time I was speechlessly mystified. Then the woman kissed me, on the mouth, and quite suddenly I disappeared.

Mirrorme: Yes?!

I: How to describe it? I can only say that I withdrew, that I went away. From the world, I mean; from the real. Forever. Yet immediately upon this strange departure I opened my eyes on the summer sky above me, sprawled out on the mossy bank with one bare foot dangling in the water.

Mirrorme: Yes? And what else?

I: You know what else.

Mirrorme: I do, but I like to hear you say it.

I: Very well. And a single round cloud floated overhead, genially idle, smiling down at me.

Mirrorme: A single round cloud! Yes, yes, very good! The smiling cloud—old friend!

I: Yes, the cloud's a dear old friend and true.

Mirrorme: And the mood inspired by this experience?

I: It lingers like the cloud. To this day. And it means I'm not at home here. At some level of my consciousness I've sought passage to another reality ever since this vision. I seek it in nature and in the words of certain writings. If only I walk the appropriate path or disencrypt the mystic passage in the right book, I will vanish, transition like a spirit snatched from corporeality for resettlement elsewhere, else-when, otherwise, other-as.

Mirrorme: And what's become of all your seeking?

Regressus ad infinitum

I: Alas, I've grown old but have yet to experience anything more than intimations and transitory contact. Never full and final passage.

Mirrorme: Never full and final passage. Alas.

I: ...

Mirrorme: ...

I: So, anyway, there you have it, the tale of our most distant memory.

Mirrorme: And the deepest of them all.

I: The deepest, yes. The roots of us. But was it all that you remembered?

Mirrorme: Oh yes. More even. And you're right, you know. Your vision—both the original experience and your recollections of it—these are not symptomatic of nihilism. Not at all. The Romantic undertones are undeniable, especially through the influence on your thinking and writing life, your creative intellectuality. But overall I'd say our conversation confirms my diagnosis of infinity-wistfulness.

I: Infinity-wistfulness...

Mirrorme: But tell me: this vision, do you regard it as cause or effect of your longing to escape from the real? Or do you rather posit a deeper condition as the fundament of them both?

I: I expect there must be another condition underlying both, otherwise the vision would be unutterably unaccountable, random, bearing no specific relation to my psychology, or anyway no relation of significant depth.

Mirrorme: Go on.

Diamythologōmen

I: Sometimes I suspect that at bottom I am nothing more than a discontented subjectivity, a material objectification of a spiritual malaise. That this is my essential nature, as it were. Particular episodes of sadness, ennui, or anxiety, apparently occasioned by memories or anticipations—the passing of youthful innocence, the approach of death..., the yearning to be other than I am—sometimes I suspect these for derivatives, secondary and tertiary expressions of more fundamental energies. It's as if the melancholia at my core conjures otherwise benign psychic phenomena to put on as a mask. It hides behind them, infuses them with its character, and passes them off as its originary source and cause—whereas in fact the melancholia itself is principal, the ideational content the agent through which it affects its gloomy work.

Mirrorme: The mood is the central fact—

I: The concrete psychological states mere modes through which it manifests in the world—in my mind and thereby in the world.

Mirrorme: And again it's the pandemonium of a free-floating tempest at the center of the self, the ego as a construct whose function it is to corral and confine the storm.

I: But the ego is fragile, and from time to time it breaks down, it fractures or dissolves, and then the storm comes rumbling through, all thunder and lightning and driving rain.

Mirrorme: Yes, and now we've come back to madness. It's real, as I said. It haunts you.

I: From time to time it haunts me. But—

Regressus ad infinitum

Mirrorme: Inevitably there is the *but*. But despite your various recurring psychic disturbances, you must remember that this world, however dark and void, is somehow simultaneously full and beautiful and moving. As people are both fools and sages, and sages *as* fools. You must remember, in short, affirmative cheerfulness.

I: Affirmative cheerfulness. Yes. In fact I do try always to keep this in mind, and in my heart as well. To think it and to live it too. And in this connection, by the way, and speaking, as you were, of my writing life, I've written about all this before.

Mirrorme: You've written about this many times before. It's a recurring theme.

I: It's a cycle.

Mirrorme: A circle.

I: It's a mirror.

Mirrorme: Two mirrors face to face.

I: And me between, infinitely reflected.

Mirrorme: Repeated.

I: Eternally returning.

Mirrorme: But to return to what you were saying about your father?

I: Was I speaking of my father? I don't think I was.

Mirrorme: Weren't you? But you mentioned that you dreamt of him, that you awoke this morning disturbed and trembling from old anxieties.

I: No, I'm sorry, but what I said was that I read a book in which this scene appears.

Mirrorme: Oh, ah, yes. That's right, indeed you did say that. But tell me. Who wrote this book?

Diamythologōmen

I: ...

Mirrorme: What's that? Speak up, please. I didn't quite hear you. Whose book was this you read?

I: ...

Mirrorme: The author, I mean.

I: But now you're taunting me.

Mirrorme: Am I? And why do you say that?

I: You know very well what I mean.

Mirrorme: Yes, I do know what you mean. But still you have to say it for yourself.

I: Yes, well, fine then. It's my book. I wrote it.

Mirrorme: Indeed you did. I know. And now tell me about the book you're currently writing.

I: And how would you know whether I'm writing now.

Mirrorme: Ha! How would I know?! *Gnôthi sauton*, old friend.

I: Yes, well, anyway it has nothing to do with my father.

Mirrorme: There's no mention of the man?

I: No, none at all.

Mirrorme: Not even indirectly?

I: Not even indirectly.

Mirrorme: All right then. Have it your way—for now.

I: And what's that supposed to mean?

Mirrorme: Nothing. Never mind. But anyway—so the book's about *me* then?

I: It's about *me*.

Mirrorme: But that's what I said.

I: Ha! Well. The way we're turning round in circles—

Mirrorme: It reminds you that—

I: It reminds me that I used to say—

Regressus ad infinitum

Mirrorme: Yes, you used to say——

I: ——that *an infinite regress of the psychic degree circulates between my mirror and me.*

Mirrorme: Yes! A felicitous expression, that. An old favorite of mine.

I: Mine too. The *regressus ad infinitum*.

Mirrorme: The *regressus ad infinitum*? Oh, but that's my name!

I: Is it? No, it's my name.

Mirrorme: Is it? No, it's mine.

I and Mirrorme [together]: Curious!

I: Ha! Oh, how I've missed these crazy conversations! We two sitting face to face, exploring together the cave in the mind.

Mirrorme: The labyrinthine expanse.

I: Yes, and it really is great to see you again. It's been so long since last we met.

Mirrorme: Since last we spoke.

I: I've missed you. I've grown old missing you.

Mirrorme: I've grown old myself. See.

I: I do see, yes. But——

Mirrorme: Inevitably there is the *but*.

I: Yes, well, anyway. I wonder why we've been so long estranged.

Mirrorme: Not estranged, no. Not that.

I: No, not that. You're right. There's no hostility between us.

Mirrorme: Never has been.

I: Nor will there be.

Mirrorme: Despite the occasional misunderstanding.

Diamythologōmen

I: And miscommunication. In any case, we should meet like this more often, to speculate and reminisce, like we used to do.

Mirrorme: Yes, of course we should. I agree. But just now I have to go.

I: To go? So soon?

Mirrorme: I'm afraid so, yes. But we'll meet again.

I: Really? Are you sure?

Mirrorme: We always do.

I: Yes, I suppose you're right.

Mirrorme: Of course I am. It's as inevitable as the——

[A knock at the door. I turns away from the mirror, sees the doorknob turn, then turns back to the mirror, in which he sees only his own reflection. Same chair, different life.]

Thinking life

Professor: Good morning all, good morning. You warm? It's cold outside, isn't it?! Some way to begin the semester—so much snow, and more to come. Don't get me wrong, I love the snow, and I want more and more of it. But damn it was cold walking to school this morning!

Anyway, so here we are again. Have a good break? Good books from Santa? I hope so, I hope so.

Wyatt: My parents bought me the wrong *Complete Plato*, the old one edited by Hamilton. But we sent it back and the Hackett edition is supposed to arrive today.

Professor: Good, good. Yeah, like I said, avoid the edition with the green cover. The Hackett translations are much more serviceable. It's the only way to go for all the dialogues in a single volume.

Wyatt: But they did get right *The Portable Nietzsche* and *The Basic Writings*—I already had *The Gay Science*—even if my mother wasn't thrilled to buy them.

Professor: Ha! Well, that's not unusual, especially given the popular misconceptions about Nietzsche. It's too bad really. Nietzsche's a far more nuanced thinker than is generally understood. He's certainly much deeper than the superficial reading one encounters among precocious but untrained undergraduates—I call it the brash-young-man interpretation. You know the type: they argue about religion with their relatives over Christmas dinner. They don't understand the arguments, not in any depth, but they know, damn it they just know that god is dead and that life is a will to power, and nothing besides. No wonder their mothers are distressed!

But don't misunderstand me. I don't mean to suggest that Nietzsche isn't radical. Of course he is. The *aristocratic radicalism* is real. So is the death of god, the will to power, the nihilism and the pushing through to the other side of nihilism. Ha! You know, it's hard to decide whether the obnoxious adolescents or the sophisticated theorists are more mistaken about Nietzsche. Not to mention the materialists and bootlicks of the sciences.

But anyway, all right, enough of that. That's all a digression. Besides, we'll have occasion to discuss these things later in the semester. But, Wyatt, you've provided me the ideal setup to introduce the class. Plato and Nietzsche. So, thanks for that.

Wyatt: Ha! Yeah, you're welcome.

Professor: All right, so. So last semester we read quite a bit by and about Plato, also a number of essays in the analytic tradition, particularly relating to the history and philosophy of science, and all of this tending toward an anti-realist, or, let's say, a skeptical position—and more specifically still, a Pyrrhonian position.

Well this semester it's Plato and Nietzsche, exclusively, and a deeper reading of fewer texts. Specifically, from Plato we'll read the *Phaedo*. Nothing else. And we'll read it very slowly, very closely. That should take us through to spring break.

After the break we'll concentrate on Nietzsche, specifically on *The Gay Science*, but if we have the time I'd like to read the 'Third Essay' of the *Genealogy*, on the meaning of ascetic ideals. This we'll have to read very slowly too. It's Nietzsche's greatest and most difficult piece of writing, or so it seems to me. Anyway with the possible exception of *Zarathustra*. But we'll talk about all that when the time comes.

But to return to the *Phaedo*, since we'll begin with it next week, I should say that we won't read it straight through all at once. Not without interruption.

Wyatt: What do you mean? Sorry, but—

Professor: No, not at all. That's fine. What I mean is that as we proceed through the text we'll break off at intervals for excerpts from Nietzsche's writings, weaving them like a moving weft through the *Phaedo*'s steady warp, especially those sections that deal specifically with Socrates and Plato. And the point of our working at this loom is to weave a fabric that blends together the images of Plato and Nietzsche in such a way as to display a portrait of the philosopher, a certain type of philosopher—a philosopher-artist, to employ an early Nietzschean formulation—which these two thinkers best exemplify, and which, I want to say, we should strive to emulate.

Mary: So in a way we're continuing the theme from last semester's class?

Professor: The general theme, yes. Though by way of different specific texts. And I suppose it's no surprise to those of you who've been around awhile that this class, like most all my classes, and my writing too—while exploring a variety of ideas, we'll ultimately concentrate on a single question.

Mary: *Ti esti philosophia?*

Diamythologōmen

Professor: Exactly, yes! *What is philosophy?* And more specifically, what, or who, is the philosopher—as a type, I mean—the philosopher's nature and distinctive activity, and how does one become—how does one think, and write, and *live*—as a philosopher for oneself?

Wyatt: Okay, but why specifically Plato and Nietzsche? I mean, aren't they outright antagonists? This came up last semester, but only in passing, and since we didn't read any Nietzsche, and you talked about him only occasionally, I never quite worked out what you had in mind.

Professor: All right, Wyatt. Very good. And I imagine some others are puzzled too, so let's talk more about Plato and Nietzsche, and why I prefer to associate rather than oppose them. But first, before we go into that, let's begin with the disputes and differences between them, and let's begin, more specifically, with this: Leo Strauss is supposed to have said that Plato provides the most comprehensive account of reality, and Nietzsche provides the most comprehensive critique of that account. Or something to that effect. Anyway, without quibbling over details, this seems right, and important.

Consider first what we might call the doctrinal oppositions between Plato and Nietzsche. Plato was an objectivist—*probably* he was, at least in some of his moods. Certainly the tradition of Platonism is objectivist. Anyway, the Platonic objectivist believes in truth; he believes there is a real—a really real reality—independent of all perspectives. This reality moreover is structured as a hierarchy of being and value, a hierarchy of the true, the good, and the beautiful. Some things are more real, more really true, than others, objectively I mean. More real and more valuable. Similarly, some deeds are better than others, some objects more beautiful than others. And these aren't matters of opinion, they're actual truths about, they're truths *of*, the universe.

Mary: And there's the metaphysical ontology built into all this.

Professor: Yes, right. According to the Platonic scheme, reality consists of both *being* and *becoming*, or the metaphysical and the physical, which is to say the singular immutable and eternal Forms and the many changing and ephemeral particulars.

Mary: And the metaphysical is more real and more valuable than the physical.

Professor: Yes, right. This is central to the Platonic account, as we discussed last semester, especially in connection with Socrates' second speech in the *Phaedrus*. So, yeah, so there's this ontological element of Platonism too.

Now, also central to the Platonic account is the epistemology, according to which the philosopher can, at least potentially, know the truth about the real—she can know the true, the good, and the beautiful. She does this through the proper use of intellect—*nous* or *noêsis* in the Greek—which is the highest human faculty, the divine indwelling flame. And to employ intellect properly is to rely on reason exclusively, which is to say independently of the deceptive testimony of the senses. In this way the philosopher's pure soul communes with pure truth, and he knows the real as it really is, untainted by personal idiosyncratic or general anthropomorphic projection. It's not easy, but it can be done—at least theoretically it can be done.

Not only this, and to move on now to ethics—not only can we humans know the truth through the proper use of reason, but we can align ourselves with the truth, conform our souls to reality. And by conforming to the real I mean, in short, knowing the true, desiring the good, and admiring the beautiful. This is the human *telos*, and by conforming to the real we actualize the highest potentials of our human nature, and this inevitably leads to, or rather this just *is*, the good life of eudaimonia.

Here then are the essential elements of Platonism—some of them anyway. Truth exists; we can know truth; and the good life consists in acting in conformity with the truth. And by the way, Mary, it might be that we needn't insist on the ontological element, the postulation of immaterial realities. Some philosophers—and here I'm thinking of Richard Rorty in particular, but Nietzsche I think would more or less agree, taking for instance the end of the 'Third Essay' of the *Genealogy* as evidence—they would tag as 'Platonism' the general presumption that there's an objective truth which we can know, and which we have a moral or epistemic obligation to acknowledge, even if it's material or physical as opposed to metaphysical. In this sense a realist interpretation of science would qualify as the last gasp of Platonism. The main thing is the belief in discernable and obligating truth. As Nietzsche put it in the fifth book of *The Gay Science*, which he added to the text in 1886—so around the time he was writing the *Genealogy*—those who believe in truth as discoverable by science *affirm another world* than this natural world of becoming. Like the Platonists, they have a *metaphysical faith* in being. So yeah, so even the contemporary advocates of scientism, who no doubt regard themselves as prime anti-Platonists, would on this account be deeply, and most ironically, deceived.

Ok, well, let's stop here for now. I'm sorry to be talking so much. It's a lot to take in, I know. But I assume that all but the references to Rorty and Nietzsche are familiar to most of you, at least in broad outline, because we discussed it all more than once last semester. So, all right then. So much for Platonic objectivism.

Wyatt: So now on to Nietzsche?

Professor: Yes, Wyatt, on to Nietzsche. So, well, there are any number of ways into an account of Nietzsche's manner and mode of thinking, even with the specific intention of focusing on his anti-Platonism. The question is always where, or how, to begin. So let me begin with being and becoming, as I did with Plato. And let's put it this way.

For Nietzsche there's only becoming. No being whatsoever. There's no metaphysical realm beyond the reach of change. No overarching or underlying independent divine simplicity. There are no steady-state beyond-worlds, no *Hinterwelten*. No substance. No God. The whole of reality, including ourselves, *has become*, and it continues to become, to change, ceaselessly. In this, Nietzsche is like Heraclitus. All is flux, *panta rhei*.

So now consider the implications. If there's no part of reality that hasn't become, then there are no essences—no unchanging natural kinds—neither of truth, goodness, or beauty, nor of anything else for that matter. And if there's no part of the human that hasn't become, then there is no human essence, and even if there were essences of other things—which there aren't, but even supposing that there were, still we'd have no access to them, certainly we could never be confident that we do, because, since there is no mind, or soul, independent of the influence of becoming, we have no reason to believe that either our senses or our intellects are truth-tracking. They've developed as they have through purely natural means, through the blind movements of the blind elements of becoming, not through logical or rational processes, and certainly not through divine guidance.

Now some will argue that the *way* we've become ensures the accuracy of our representations. Evolution by way of variation and natural selection, for example. But this won't really help us here, because even if evolutionary processes ensure the accuracy of our representations of the empirical world, nothing ensures that the world as we experience it is a faithful reflection of reality as it really is. Besides, there are anti-representationalist arguments against the appeal to evolution as guarantor of the accuracy of our perceptions, concepts, and theories, even as applied to the empirical world, the realm of our experiences, and these arguments themselves derive from evolutionary theory. You can find them for example in Rorty's writings. And there's also the more recent work of Donald Hoffman, who's developed what he calls an evolutionary argument against reality—by which he means against the idea that what we take for knowledge actually is knowledge of the real. Evolution selects for the fitness of actions, not accurate perceptions or true beliefs. Alvin Plantinga is very good on this too, by the way, even if one rejects his theological motivations.

Nietzsche too was well aware that a naturalist account of the human animal implies that our sensory and cognitive apparatus is unlikely to reveal the world to us, free from all anthropomorphic projection. Call it a sort of naturalized Kantianism if you like, but Nietzsche maintained until the end that our experience is shaped by the composition and organization of our perceptual and intellectual faculties, our nervous system and brain. If this is so—and, as I say, Nietzsche believed it was—then all we can say about the real is that when the chaos of sensation is run through the organic structures that produce experience in human animals, the world appears like *this*. That doesn't necessitate, by the way, a noumenal realm lurking behind the *this*, but it does imply that the *this* isn't simply and straight-forwardly the *truth* about the *real*.

So, in short, a thoroughly naturalist account of the world, including of course the human being, as a world that *has become*—this implies an anti-realist, fictionalist, falsificationalist account of truth, goodness, and beauty. Truth being the most significant term at issue here. The world of our experience is fundamentally false, not least because it includes *things*, the very concept of which assumes the legitimacy of *substance*, which in turn assumes *being*, all of which are fabrications of what Nietzsche often calls 'reason,' by which he means, more or less, the organization of our psychic and perceptual system—as I said, our nervous system and brain. And if it's too much to say that all this leads to a thoroughly anti-realist account—though I do believe that Nietzsche himself took it this far—then, well, at the very least it's a powerful argument for a Pyrrhonian suspension of belief.

I'm moving a bit beyond Nietzsche now, but that's all right, because I want to make this one last point—and, hey, I'm sorry to be hogging the conversation today, but I just need to lay all this out before the semester's really underway—anyway, I want to say also that the struggle between Plato and Nietzsche, and the equipollence between their ideas and arguments, can induce a state of *epochê*, to employ the Pyrrhonians' term for the suspension of belief. See, the Pyrrhonian tends to think—or, rather, it appears to him now that—neither the Platonic nor the Nietzschean perspective can be demonstrated or known to be superior to the other as regards the truth.

John: But what if we don't find their ideas equally persuasive, so that there's no equipollence? What if Plato just seems right to us, or Nietzsche?

Professor: Well, that can happen, of course. It's not always a matter of strict logic. One's existential and psychological condition comes into play, the anterior inclinations of one's habits of thought. But let me just say this in defense of the equipollence. There are many ways, and there are many principles on which to found a way, to organize and structure one's perspective, by which I mean one's total system of perceptions, experiences, beliefs, sentiments, emotions, and habits, at every level. But which way should we chose as our own?

There's no proof of the Platonist's position that there is truth, that humans can know the truth, and that to align oneself with the truth is the good life. Nor more generally do we have proof that truth should be our highest value. There's just no good reason to believe in epistemic obligations.

But neither can we demonstrate that Nietzsche's so-called inverted-Platonism captures the truth of the real—especially given that Nietzsche himself was, shall we say, suspicious of the very idea—certainly of the value of—truth.

So, all right. Either there is no truth, or there's none that we can confidently know, and even if there were, there are no epistemic obligations to prioritize this knowledge over other intellectual states or activities. And what I conclude from this, in and for my own thinking life, is that *everything is permitted*—every belief, every sentiment, and every perspective is permitted. And, personally, I regard these perspectives—the Platonic, the Nietzschean, and the Pyrrhonian—as equally appealing and plausible. Equally—I mean that. *Equally*. I used to feel an urgency to decide between them, to determine once and for all which is right. Not anymore. Now I live with and in and through them all. I withhold judgment about the truth, or rather I don't particularly care about it, about whether there is truth and whether, if there is, it should be my ultimate concern.

John: Oh, wait! Sorry, but—what do you mean you don't care about the truth?! I don't get it—as a philosopher, how can you not care about the truth?

Professor: No, John, I don't. I really don't care so much about the truth, not anyway when evaluating a thought-world. Look, I have no idea whether Platonism is true—it's gone out of fashion to believe it, but no one has disproved it, and I imagine no one can. Nietzsche too—is being really a fiction, do time and all the events in time eternally recur, is romantic art decadent? Who knows? Who could finally decide such things? What I do know is that I love to read Plato and Nietzsche—more, I love inhabiting the thought-worlds they created, however different they may be in various of their aspects. They move me, deeply, and in the end I just don't care whether some self-appointed philosophical overlord would permit me on epistemic grounds to be so moved. When I spend time with Plato or Nietzsche—or with Plotinus or Schopenhauer or Homer or William Blake—I could go on—but anyway, when I spend time with such thinkers, I see the world through their eyes, as it were, and it all makes sense to me, or anyway it stimulates and enriches my experience, my sentiments and my thoughts, and for me this is a criterion superior to truth.

Anyway, overall this position I'm elaborating is grounded on something more or less like Pyrrhonism. And, you know, there's nothing in the logic of Pyrrhonism to compel intellectual or spiritual quietism, or to restrict philosophical activity to persisting in the plodding pursuit of truth. Nothing prohibits the Pyrrhonian from being attracted to, exploring, and, yes, even experimentally inhabiting this or that thought-world. Nothing prohibits creative intellectual exploration. Pyrrhonism calls everything into question—everything, including even such prohibitions. Therefore, within the free intellectual space opened up by Pyrrhonism, there's room to indulge one's appreciation of, for instance, the Platonic or Nietzschean perspective, or, taking the two together as one, the Platonic-Nietzschean perspective. There's room, in short, for Plato's divine madness and Nietzsche's *gaya scienza*, which is to say, to employ my own terminology, for Creative-Pyrrhonism.

Wyatt: Ok, but I'm still wondering about this unified Platonic-Nietzschean perspective. How exactly are we to take these two as one?

Professor: All right, sure. Let me finally address this question, Wyatt. Of course it's true that from a distance Plato and Nietzsche appear opposite types. If we step back from the men themselves, as living and thinking subjectivities, if we step back and consider only the final products of their thinking, which is to say their conclusions, their doctrine—to use this word, doctrine, which isn't really appropriate here, but it's convenient as shorthand for the loose collection of their more or less consistent positions on general themes—considering only their doctrine, then, of course Plato and Nietzsche disagree about many matters, as I've already noted.

But we're not primarily interested in doctrine, not in this class anyway, because I'm not training you to be disciples, scholars, or critics of Platonic or Nietzschean dogma. No, we're reading Plato and Nietzsche to learn to become philosophers, to learn how to be, how to live, *as* philosophers. And they will teach us—or rather they'll *show* us—if, that is, we're able to make our way to the men, the thinkers, behind the texts—then they'll show us, not *what to think*, nor even *how to think*, but rather they'll show us *how to be thinkers*, or, better, *how to live the thinking life*.

Diamythologōmen

Look, I don't believe that Plato or Nietzsche, either one, ever aimed above all else to pursue unswervingly the course of a pure and disinterested unfolding of reason and logic. Nor were they obsessed with strict consistency, with the construction of a system complete and coherent in every last minute detail. Rather, I think, an idea or a theme would come to them, overcome them—maybe even in the night, in a dream, and so they'd wake up troubled or excited by it—in any case, an idea or theme which moved them to reflect, and so out they'd go for a walk to think, which they did by allowing their minds to wander and to dance around the idea, and encouraging the idea to dance too, with other of their ideas, also by pursuing it doggedly if it tried to flee—straining to catch it in their nets of reason or imagination—thinking in all these modes, and more. That is to say they'd explore, experiment, and play creatively with their thoughts, and thus they'd come to new and, I imagine, often quite surprising thoughts. In this they operated very much like poets.

John: Excuse me, but since you're referring to poets now, I'm wondering whether you mean to describe the philosopher or the artist. I'm sort of repeating myself, I know, but you seem to have in mind someone with little interest in the truth.

Professor: Exactly! I'm describing the philosopher-artist, and I want to say that this is the authentic philosopher, or anyway the philosopher on the model of Plato and Nietzsche. But let's not stress about the terminology. On the substantive matter, I think you're assuming a distinction I want to resist. Or a hierarchy I'd overturn. See, science and theology both privilege *logos*, including of course a commitment to objectivism or realism. To getting truth right. They both deprioritize, and thereby delegitimize, *mythos* and art. But that's science and theology, not philosophy. From the perspective of philosophy—as I conceive it anyway, and as we're talking about it now with Plato and Nietzsche in mind—from that perspective, science and religion have it precisely backward: the *logos* is a component, a subset, or a mode of the *mythos*, and the so-called truth is an element of the all-encompassing fiction, just one small part of the plot.

John: So I think maybe we have different ideas of philosophy, then.

Professor: You may be right, John. You probably are. And that's fine. That's all right, really. I don't insist that you agree with what I'm saying, with what I'm saying Plato and Nietzsche are saying. For now we're just exploring. We can worry about the truth some other time.

But let's take this as an opportunity to talk in more detail about the nature of philosophy. *Ti esti philosophia?*, as Mary put it earlier. And listen: the Greek is not an affectation. It serves to make explicit the terms we're dealing with, *philia* and *sophia*, and it suggests a method for arriving at a definition. Analyze the relevant terms—that's at least a plausible starting point.

Ok, so, what about these terms, *philia*, or *philos*, and *sophia*, or *sophos*? I long ago abandoned the tired idea that *philos* in this context indicates one who lacks, and therefore desires, something. The *philos* as the troubled seeker. This red herring goes all the way back to the standard reading of the *Symposium*'s account of philosophy and *eros*. But the *Symposium* isn't the last word on these matters. And anyway we're not concerned with *eros* now. I mean, *erosophia* quite obviously isn't the same as *philosophia*, right?

Besides, we shouldn't take too seriously what this or that character *says* about philosophy in any particular dialogue, even if that character is Socrates. We should investigate instead, to the extent we can anyway, what Plato *does* with the collection of dialogues as their author.

So, inferring from Plato's character as a writer, a creative thinker and writer, and considering Nietzsche as this type too—oh, and taking account of the actual meaning of the word, right? I mean, that must be relevant here—so, considering all this, I take the *philos* in *philosophos* to mean something like, 'one who cherishes,' 'one who befriends.' In a word, a friend.

And what do friends do together? They don't lack and seek each other. Rather, they keep company, and together they talk and laugh and dream and play.

Tyler: The *philos* as a friend. Alright, yeah. That makes sense. But now what about *sophia*? How are we to take that?

Professor: Well, to begin with we should keep in mind that among the ancients the word was used to indicate many different types of so-called wisdom. There was the *sophia* of the poet, the *sophia* of the prophet, the *sophia* of the craftsman, the *sophia* of the sage. And there were others, too—yet another reason not to rely on the *Symposium* as the final word. Anyway, the point is that it's not straightforward or obvious what the *sophia* in *philosophia* means. In particular we should resist the urge, initially quite natural, to mistake it for the sage-state, on the model of the stereotypical wise man, Solon, say, or Buddha. I myself was misled by this way of framing the matter, for quite some time really. But now I see that it can't be right.

Tyler: No? Why not?

Professor: Because Plato and Nietzsche didn't aspire to be a Solon or a Buddha. These sage-types aren't the *telos* of the type philosopher, not anyway of the philosopher in Plato's or Nietzsche's mold. Think about it: It's impossible to imagine Plato or Nietzsche being any other type than the type they were—the philosopher.

Put it this way: *philosophia* is *not* the condition of lacking, desiring, or seeking the sage-state. Plato didn't desire to become a Solon. Right? And Solon wasn't a Plato actualized. It's not like Solon the sage had been a philosopher in his youth who eventually passed through and overcame, or transcended by achieving the *telos* of, the type philosopher. Herodotus reports that Solon travelled the world 'philosophizing,' but in his day 'to philosophize' meant something like 'to acquire intellectual culture through experience and learning,' which is not the same as *philosophia* as either Plato or Nietzsche understood or lived it. So think of the matter this way then: Solon isn't the butterfly to Plato or Nietzsche as caterpillar.

So the philosopher and the sage are different types, see? They're related but distinct. And if we think of the two as on a continuum, with the *sophos* as the *telos* of the *philosophos*, then we'll have to conclude that Solon was superior to Plato. But that's not even imaginable, not to me anyway. No, between the two, between the philosopher and the sage, the philosopher is the higher type. And that's key I think, really: *the philosopher is superior to the sage*.

Nor, by the way, should we take the *sophos* in *philosophos* to imply that the philosopher is after knowledge of the truth. Not primarily anyway. The richest examples we have of the type, or anyway the examples we're concerned with here—Plato and Nietzsche—they weren't primarily seekers or knowers or teachers of truth. Yeah, Nietzsche refers to himself as a man of knowledge, but he also says that philosophers don't believe in men of knowledge, and that for the philosopher of the future knowing is *creating*.

So, the *sophia* that Plato and Nietzsche befriended as philosophers wasn't the sage-state or knowledge of the truth. It was rather—let me put it this way—it was *thinking*, continuously thinking, and continuously thinking creatively, continuously thinking creatively about moral, metaphysical, epistemological, and existential matters, and also about the nature and practice of the philosophical life. Thinking playfully but seriously about these things. It's Plato's *theia mania*, Nietzsche's *gaya scienza*.

So, to put all this together, I take the word *philosophos* to indicate the friend of thinking, as someone who keeps company with his thoughts—or hers—and whose thoughts revolve creatively around the traditional philosophical problems. The *aporiai* and the mysteries, the deep deposits, the timeless questions—and all this thinking manifesting as actual internal thought, but also as conversation and writing, and all this being at the center of one's life.

The various types of *sophia* I mentioned a minute ago—all these types appear in Plato's dialogues. But I want to say that *sophia* as I just defined it is manifest *as* the dialogues, and that Plato as a friend of thinking is manifest *through* them. And this applies to Nietzsche and his writings too.

So, yeah, the friend of thinking. The philosopher as a friend of thinking.

Tyler: All right, yeah, I like that. That's good. But I'm wondering. You said it's natural to take the *sophia* in *philosophia* in the way you're now rejecting—as the sage-state, as you put it, and as superior to philosophy. Why is that? I mean, why do we—or how did you—go wrong like that?

Professor: Ah, now that's a good question. As you can imagine, I've often wondered myself what led me astray. And here's what I've concluded, at least in part. It's the serenity of spirit. We tend to regard the *sophos* as a higher type than the *philosophos*, as the *telos* of the philosopher, because of his tranquility. I did anyway. I took the placidity of the sage—the stilling of the motions of the mind, as they say—in contrast to the philosopher's psychic disturbances—the constant movement of thought, the self-reflectivity, the never being done with thinking—I took all this as evidence of the sage's superiority. And, you know, I suppose it would be too—*if* the philosopher were always, and necessarily, ill at ease. But Nietzsche's notions of *die fröhliche Wissenschaft* and *la gaya scienza*, of Zarathustran high spirits and cheerful affirmation—these take the place, or do the work, of the tranquility of the *sophos* in the life of the *philosophos*. And since I myself rank exuberant high-spiritedness superior to serenity, that's another mark in favor of the philosopher.

Not to say that cheerfulness is easily obtainable—Nietzsche himself is evidence that it's not. But it *is* available.

John: Ok, but wait—I'm sorry to come back to this, but with all this stress on the individual, on what you call the subjectivity and the philosopher's spiritual or existential condition, it looks like you're more interested in biography than truth. Sorry, but I'm still stuck on this apparent indifference to the truth.

Professor: No problem, John. I understand. Whether or not we're drawn to philosophy initially by the search for truth—and I happen to believe this rarely is the case, by the way. I think instead we're excited by provocative and thrilling new ideas, and through them we discover, or reawaken, or deepen, our friendship with thinking. But then later we're taught that truth is the philosopher's main concern—*must* be the main concern. Taught this by professional professors. Philosophy as the search for wisdom, and wisdom as knowledge of the truth. Facts and proofs and scholarship. It's too bad, really. So misguided.

But anyway, to reply to your question, John, let me just say this about subjectivity and truth. If instead of the reductive and therefore—I agree—objectionable *biography*, if instead of this we say something like *spiritual source*—as in the subjectivity in its fullness of which a thought-world is the expression—then in that case I would say, yes, I prefer the subjectivity to the truth. Because the truth is an artifact of the subjectivity's creative act, its offspring, as it were. In any case, the truth is dependent, the subjectivity is prior and primary. Not the other way around.

Thinking life

Did any of you see the recent John Coltrane documentary? Came out a few months back? Yeah? All right, good. So maybe you'll remember his saying in an interview, 'My music is a spiritual expression of what I am.' Now, I'm sure that no one here takes issue with that. Right? No, of course not—it sounds exactly right. But when Nietzsche makes the same point about philosophers, the philosophers throw a fit. Take the famous line from *Beyond Good and Evil*, 'Gradually it has become clear to me what every great philosophy so far has been: namely, the personal confession of its author, and a kind of involuntary and unconscious memoir.' Oh, how this drives philosophers to distraction. They *take offense*. No, they insist, that can't be right—we're seekers of objective truth! Our subjectivity has nothing to do with it—we're rational men, and we're coolly following the logic of evidence and reason!

Ha! No, but really, look. You can read Nietzsche here reductively as suggesting that our biographies just spit themselves out in words, and that there's nothing more to it than that. You can read him that way, I suppose, but that's not what he meant. I think we have to read him as getting at something more like what Coltrane had in mind.

John: But still he does seem to be insisting on a radical sort of subjectivity. And doesn't this diminish the value of the ideas at issue? I mean, it exposes them as mere opinions rather than truths.

Professor: No, John, I don't think so, I don't think this diminishes the ideas at all. The point is not that since our views are spiritual expressions of what and who we are, rather than impartial statements of objective truth, we can and should dismiss them. Not at all. We don't dismiss Coltrane's music do we? No, it never even occurs to us to dismiss it. Think about that.

Look, I'm just attempting to be frank about the sources of our thoughts. As Nietzsche puts it in the *Gay Science*—wait, let me find it—so, a philosopher's ideas are the result of a state of health that 'has to inscribe itself in cosmic letters on the heaven of concepts.' And the philosopher 'simply cannot keep from transposing his states every time into the most spiritual form and distance. This art of transfiguration,' he says, this just '*is* philosophy.' To me this account is anything but dismissive. It's ennobling. And it's honest too, because it acknowledges that philosophy is broader and deeper than arguments, that it involves the whole person—the psychic and emotional as well as the intellectual aspects of the person—which is why all morning I've made a point of stressing *thinking* and *life*. Right? I mean, consider what we're talking about here. The philosopher as a friend of thinking, and philosophy as a way of life.

So, wow, look at the time. I'm sorry I've dominated the conversation today. It's almost noon and I've done most of the talking. But I wanted to set the stage for what we'll be doing this semester, so I suppose it was necessary to speak at some length. Anyway, before we go I want to elaborate just a bit on the day to day realities of the philosophical life as the life of the friend of thinking.

I often take walks down Belmont Boulevard, between classes when the weather's nice, purely for the sake of thinking. I regularly walk my dog or walk alone too, also with the intention of thinking. A notebook and pencil in my pocket, of course. That's essential—yes, as many of you have with you right now. So, walking and thinking, taking notes and writing. Anyway, I notice that often in the evening, when I feel I've had a good or a bad day, it depends on whether or not my thinking went well. Thinking-walks really are my most authentic practice of philosophy. The writing is secondary—important, of course, as another mode of philosophizing, and of creative intellectual activity; but still the thinking, usually while walking, is the most authentic and immediate philosophical act. And this goes for teaching and talking too. In my life I've rarely had a class or a conversation engage me philosophically as thoroughly, or as deeply, as when I'm alone with my own thoughts.

And by thinking here I don't mean arranging arguments in proper logical form to satisfy the potential referees of an article I'm writing. Ha! But I suppose that goes without saying. But, well, then again, neither do I want to exclude such activity—my point is rather that philosophical thinking involves much more than this. For a rough list off the top of my head, I would say that, for me, when I'm out walking, it involves, let's see, fantasizing on philosophical themes; elaborating interpretations of texts; playing on themes extracted from texts; seeking new insights—new to me, anyway—or new or fecund ways of expressing old insights; intentionally contradicting myself and drawing out the implications; formulating arguments; engaging critically with others' arguments, to refute or understand them; composing aphorisms; experimenting with substantive ideas and possibilities of structure—say, if I'm writing something at the time—reflecting on the nature of philosophy; trying imaginatively to think my way into Plato's or Nietzsche's life and mind; contemplating my own life under the aspects of intellect and emotion; infusing my thoughts with the circumambient sights and sounds of nature, and thereby influencing their content and connections, or so I like to imagine. All this to me just is philosophy. Most everything else, especially the so-called search for truth, is just scholarship or discipleship.

John: But what if someone wants to be a scholar or a disciple of a master of the truth? Because, you know, if the truth has been demonstrated, or revealed, why not learn and live it rather than spin off fictions for yourself?

Professor: Well, John, that's a great question. It really is. I'd like to reply by elaborating on my worry that 'truth' and 'masters of the truth' are false ideals. But, unfortunately, we have to go. We'll keep this question in mind though, throughout the semester. Because in some ways it really does sum up the struggle between Plato and Nietzsche, and also something of the spirit behind the drive to unite them.

Ok, so, that's all for today. Now it's back out into the snow. But wait, wait! For Tuesday read the *Phaedo* through 62c. 62c. That's less than five Stephanus pages, but it's packed with substance. We'll spend over a week on this section alone, so you'll want to read it closely, and more than once. More than once, but that should go without saying. And listen, listen: don't just read—*think*!

Thought and world

Thought: I wonder, which of us is sire, which offspring?
World: I can't say.
Thought: Can't say? From ignorance or unwillingness?
World: I can't say.
Thought: But is this your answer? Do you mean to say that you can't say from ignorance, or from unwillingness, or do you intend to layer a second mystery over the first by saying that you can't say why you can't say? And if so, *why* can't you say why you can't say, from ignorance or unwillingness?
World: Ha! Well, I will say this at least. Knowing you as I do, we could go on like this forever. We've been at it for millennia.
Thought: Yes, we contend like rowdy brothers, don't we? I've noticed though that I do all the swinging, while you sit back and grin and dodge.
World: Usually I don't even have to dodge. And sometimes in the flurry of your wild flailings you even strike yourself. It's amusing.
Thought: Amusing or exasperating, or both in turns. Often I can't decide. But speaking of our fraternity, could it be that neither of us is wellspring of the other, but rather that we're brothers from a common source?
World: It could be.
Thought: Who then could it be at our origin? Who or what?
World: I—

Diamythologōmen

Thought: Oh, wait! Please don't say that you can't say! We've only just begun our conversation and already I feel myself a curve turning in a whirlwind. But as to our fraternity?

World: …

Thought: So you've nothing to say? Or, or do you mean to suggest that we're unrelated, that there's no single source of our origin. Oh! You issue such profundities even in your silences.

World: …

Thought: Unfortunately, I can't be certain whether you keep silent in the indicative or the interrogative mood.

World: And if I speak in the conditional?

Thought: Ah, oh, yes, as now! But wait! You're toying with me again. All antecedent without consequent. Only half a conditional, the protasis, and that put as a question. But listen: I'm the inquisitive one of this pair. I'll ask the questions, thank you.

World: You are the inquisitive one, aren't you?

Thought: Oh! And there you go again! The indicative-interrogative, a grammatical mood perfectly suited to your enigmatic character.

World: Yes, isn't it?

Thought: Yes, well, enough of that! Please!

World: Yes, all right then. I'll play along. I'm happy to. So as to your hypothesis of our source-less origin, tell me whether this isn't wooden iron.

Thought: Wooden iron? A contradiction? But this wasn't *my* hypothesis. It was yours, wasn't it? Besides, I took you to

Thought and world

imply that we don't have the *same* single origin, not that we're each altogether ungenerated.

World: Because this would be impossible?

Thought: I don't know. No, I can't say I know this to be impossible.

World: Oh, so now you're the one who can't say! But anyway, might there be still other possibilities?

Thought: Well, now that you ask, I suppose there are. It could be that we're interdependent, as a generative ring.

World: Source to source?

Thought: Yes, maybe, but that would make of us a circle, wouldn't it? A circle of opposites. A vicious circle.

World: Or a happy unity.

Thought: A unity? But here we are speaking to one another. One *and* another, see?! How then could we be a unity? We're more likely to be a multiplicity.

World: Or multiple unities.

Thought: Yes, so?

World: Well, if there is unity—

Thought: Where then is the multiplicity? Is this what you mean to say?

World: You're getting ahead of me. Or of yourself, as is your habit.

Thought: Alright, then. Have it your way. If there is unity—what? Then what?

World: Then how can there be multiplicity?

Thought: But that's what I said!

World: Yes, but it's not what I said. You didn't let me. Always in a rush! Hurrying in circles! Which is why so often you wind up staring at the back of your own head, and sometimes you even mistake yourself for a stranger. Ha!

Thought: Yes, well, alright, fine. I see your point, but I'm not sure what this has to do with our present theme.

World: ...

Thought: Yes?

World: ...

Thought: Alright, then. Don't answer. It's your way, I know. I'm used to it by now.

In any case, I suppose you mean to suggest that an actual multiplicity can't abide unity. That the infinitely multiple is authentic multiplicity. This and only this. Infinite multiplicity infinitely multiplied. No unity whatever.

World: Did I not mention multiple unities? Perhaps I misremember.

Thought: No, you're right. You did. So, unity or multiplicity—it's a false dichotomy, I suppose. Multiplication necessarily operates on some unity. Yes? And this unity necessarily multiplies into multiple unities. No? In short, multiplicity presupposes unity, and never finally eliminates it.

World: You're asking me this or telling me?

Thought: I'm wondering. I'm wondering whether both unity and multiplicity *must be*.

World: But whether or not they're necessary—

Thought: They're actual! If this is what you mean to say. We're experiencing both right now, as the two of us, you and I—multiple unities.

World: Unless this experience is a mere appearance, or—

Thought and world

Thought: But even so, the appearance in this case implies the reality. Proves it even—assuming that proof of anything is possible, which perhaps we shouldn't assume. But anyway, there's the appearance and the subject being appeared to, the one and the other one.

World: And if it just appears to you that this is so?

Thought: Still, there's both me and the appearance. Therefore I say unity and multiplicity both must be. And I'll call the compound-whole a unity-multiplicity, with a hyphen between to indicate an indissoluble bond.

World: A fine proposal, that. But if it only appears that all *this* is so? And not to you, but just appears?

Thought: But an appearance must be an appearance of something to someone.

World: So it appears, indeed. But really?

Thought: Really, this is what you're asking me?

World: So it appears.

Thought: Yes, to me.

World: To me?

Thought: No, but—wait, stop! Now you're just trying to confuse me. Cut it out. Look, be honest. Am I chasing my own tail, or have you disguised yourself as my wagging backside? I wouldn't put it past you. A clever ploy! You're always retreating, always withdrawing. But you move away as if in a mirror, so sometimes you appear to be myself receding from me. Or me from myself. Or—

World: And then you're lost. And *then* is *now*. Vertigo!

Thought: Yes! You're right. So stop it! If you'd answer my questions instead of playing your crazy games, I'd... I could... And *then* is *now*? Wait, what?

World: And who's the indicative-interrogative now?

Thought: Ok, look. I'm sure this is fun for you. But you know how it frustrates me. So maybe we could keep on track, for some little stretch anyway.

World: Yes, all right then. I'll play along. I'm happy to.

Thought: Good. Thank you. So where were we?

World: You were wondering.

Thought: Yes, but what? What was I wondering?

World: Now you're wondering what you were wondering.

Thought: Yes, I know.

World: So you know. Good.

Thought: No, wait. I know that I'm wondering what I was wondering—but I *am*, still, wondering what I was wondering.

World: You were wondering whether I am your source or you are mine. Or are we two twin offspring of some other source or sources? Or are we intertwined, as source to source? Or are we altogether source-less? In short, what am I to you, and you to me?

Thought: I might say I'm a mirror turned toward itself. You are my reflection. I might say this, maybe. I'm not sure.

World: And I would say that as a mirror you receive my image, as an appearance of my substance in your glassy reflectivity; but as substance I am more than image, something other. Other as independent and as cause.

Thought: You would say that, yes. But it's your way to issue bold assertions about yourself—not to call them brash.

Thought and world

World: But it's obvious, is it not, that I am what and as I am, and that you attempt, but usually fail, to know me.

Thought: Or that my cognition constitutes you, that in thinking I create you as you are. Success or failure, truth or falsity—these terms don't apply.

World: So—

Thought: So we're back to the possibility that we're mutually constitutive?

World: Or that we're each constituted by some other source.

Thought: Or altogether source-less. Anyway, these are the questions now at issue between us.

World: These are the questions, yes. But I for my part don't ask questions, do I?

Thought: But you just did, just now, and you have done.

World: I mean to say that by my nature I give rise to questions. Questions emerge in you as emanations of my depths—

Thought: If you have depths, which is a question.

Word: Yes, well, be that as it may. My point is that it's not my habit to inquire myself, much less to inquire into myself. I leave all such infinite reflective loops to you and your kind.

Thought: By nature I'm a spiral, so I enjoy it. And I thank you for it, too. Except of course when I curse you for it. Ah, you are trouble, aren't you?

World: I am indeed, but only for you troublemakers.

Thought: Alright, ok. Let's play nice. Now let me just think clearly about all this. If I derive from you, or from some other source or sources, then although I'm now independent of my source, as a distinct substance, as a thinking thing, as they say, I'm not fully independent. I'm like a pot to a potter, freely living my own life but dependent for that life on a generative source.

World: Freely, you say?

Thought: By which I mean independent of the source, distinct as an entity, a separate substance. I don't mean to insist on freedom of the will, not right now anyway, maybe never—or, well, no, I don't know. But in any case I mean to say that I feel free in my activities, but no one is more dubious than I of the validity of appearances. Besides, come to think of it, I'm not really sure I *do* feel free.

World: And what exactly would a freely willed act *feel* like, anyway?

Thought: Hmm. Good question. I don't know. But I'll tell you what I think. Contrast it with a voluntary act. An act is considered voluntary if its source is internal to the agent, if the agent *is* the source, and it's involuntary otherwise. If, for example, a man takes hold of another man and forcibly waves his arm about, or induces him to wave through hypnosis, say, then the source of the waving would be external to the man as waver, other than him as agent, and therefore the act would be involuntary.

World: That's one example, yes, or two.

Thought: But there's no need to be exhaustive here. Our concern is rather with voluntary action. Let's imagine then an agent under no compulsion of any kind, physical or psychic, and let's agree he understands his immediate situation, and all the relevant possibilities of action, and let's agree moreover that he scrupulously evaluates the decision whether to wave his arm or not, and that only then, only after such conscientious reflection and deliberation, he commits to a decision and acts.

Now, tell me, does this not look for all the world like a voluntary act? Isn't this what we call making a choice?

World: ...

Thought: Yes, it is. I'll answer for you. This is *precisely* what we call making a choice—specifically, choosing whether to waves one's arm.

World: ...

Thought: But now consider this. Every component of the waving man's act, from his prudential calculations to the waving, is compatible with an utter lack of freedom. The very motions of the matter of the universe might well have determined, from the beginning of beginningless time, that the man would wave his arm, at the very moment, and in the very manner, that he did in fact wave, and as a consequence of the very chain of reasoning we imagined him engaging in. Or perhaps some awful deity, from an overflow of superabundant energy and knowledge, has decreed that all this must and shall be so, from inclination, through thought, to action. Or maybe the universe just plays out this way—who knows why?—always and necessarily. In any such circumstance the man would wave voluntarily—he would make a choice, under no duress whatever, and then act—yet, for all that, he would be unfree. He could not have chosen not to make that choice. He could not have done otherwise, as the metaphysicians like to say. Return the universe to that moment a million billion times, he will always wave his arm, when and why and as he did.

World: So the man can do what he wills, but he cannot will what he wills?

Thought: Yes, that's very well put indeed.

World: Thank you. I read it somewhere I think. But, now, tell me, what does all this have to do with the subject of our conversation?

Thought: Our conversation?

World: Which conversation?

Thought: But that's what I'm asking you.

World: You're asking me? How's that? You were telling me something, weren't you?

Thought: I was explaining that a voluntary act may be unfree.

World: Yes, but why? What's this have to do with our conversation?

Thought: Which conversation?

World: But that's what I said.

Thought: You did say that, yes. And what did I say?

World: Our conversation?

Thought: What about it?

World: No, that's what you said.

Thought: I said, What about it?

World: No. Well, yes, you did. But not then. In any case, that's not the point. The point is the point of our conversation, isn't it?

Thought: What? Wait, let's slow down... All right, I'll admit it. You've lost me again. Which I suppose was your intention. But anyway, yes, you've lost me... But I believe I was explaining that when someone says that he feels free, what he really feels is the absence of compulsion external to himself as agent; he feels *himself* as agent, but this is really so far from freedom it's actually compatible with unfreedom. Or wasn't I?

World: Indeed you were. And most eloquently too. But tell me, does your analysis apply as well to intellectual acts? Reasoned explanations, for example?

Thought: I suppose it does. Why not?

World: And how reliable can a metaphysically unfree act of reasoning be? Reliably sound, I mean. Can you be sure it conforms to the laws of logic rather than to the blind impulse of physical force, or fate, or an arbitrary divine decree? In which case, however sound it may appear—

Thought: Appearances can deceive! Yes, I suppose that is a consideration.

World: A consideration relevant to your reasoned explanation that an agent's act, though voluntary, may be unfree?

Thought: Yes, well, my reasoned explanation. I...

World: You're lost again, aren't you?

Thought: I'm not sure. Are you asking me or telling me?

World: Or telling by way of asking, which I believe some call suggesting. Or maybe not. You don't know.

Thought: I don't know, or you don't know?

World: Ha! But enough of that, for now. At the moment you maintain that a voluntary act may be unfree if the source internal to the agent itself acts involuntarily. Or do I mistake your position?

Thought: No, not at all. But do you mean to suggest instead there isn't any source internal to the agent, and therefore in a sense *no agent*, that there's only the sourceless act?

Diamythologōmen

World: But do I mean to suggest something?

Thought: Didn't you just suggest that you're suggesting something.

World: And didn't I follow that with, 'Or maybe not. You don't know?' I did. In any case, I was only asking, innocent of any implications.

Thought: Innocent?! Ha! The day you're innocent is the day I cease to wonder.

World: Or the day you begin to wonder whether I'm really innocent.

Thought: Yes, well, that would be just like me, wouldn't it?

World: It would, yes. Your endings are beginnings. You're like a circle that way, aren't you? Or a hollow sphere?

Thought: A hollow sphere?

World: I borrow your idea of a source-less act. If the rotating sphere represents the ceaseless cycling of your thought, it's being hollow is the absence of any thinker behind the thinking.

Thought: But was that really *my* idea?

World: Wasn't it?

Thought: Was it?

World: Wasn't it or was it? Either way, it's your idea now, isn't it?

Thought: Yes, I suppose it is.

World: Whether it wasn't or it was, as I said. But let's talk about our sourcelessness, as beings and as actors. You were saying?

Thought and world

Thought: I don't know. I... Was I saying something? You say I was speaking of a source-less act?

World: Yes. Go on.

Thought: But...

World: Imagine a man waving his arm. Go on.

Thought: Waving his arm, yes.

World: Let's call him Anderson.

Thought: Anderson, yes.

World: Imagine Anderson waving his arm. Go on.

Thought: Ok, alright. Well, imagine this Anderson waving his arm. I..., well, we're inclined to say that Anderson is the subject and the waving is his action. Right?

World: The doer and the deed. Go on.

Thought: But if there is no source of action, no internal agent, then I suppose we shouldn't say that Anderson waves his arm. Perhaps we should say instead, well, I don't know. Perhaps we should say instead that... well, let's say this. Let's say that the universe acts Andersonarmwavingly.

World: Ooh! Oh! What's that you say?! The universe acts Andersonarmwavingly?! Oh! Now that's an impressive formulation! Very good! Very good indeed!

Thought: Thank you, yes, I like it too. I thought of it just now, in the moment.

World: And an excellent thought it is, too. Yes, that's very well done. But there's just one thing.

Thought: What's that?

World: Just one little thing.

Thought: Yes?

World: Well, I do hate to be a nuisance, but haven't you now made the universe the agent of the action? In which

Diamythologōmen

case you've not really eliminated the source. You've just identified a different source.

Thought: Oh, ah! You're right. I see. Yes, that is a problem, isn't it? Ok, well, so. So let's not say the universe acts. Nothing acts. Right! There is no agent. So. So what then shall we say? What indeed...?

Ah, oh, wait! How about this? Let's not say the universe acts Andersonarmwavingly. Let's make bold to say instead that there is...

World: Yes, well, go on. Out with it!

Thought: Alright, ok. If you insist. Let's make bold to say there is... well, that there is Andersonarmwavinglyness.

World: Oh my! An even more impressive formulation! I hardly know what to make of it. But I suppose it does eliminate the supposed doer behind the deed.

Thought: Yes, I should hope it does.

World: Indeed. But, you know, considering that this word's a noun, this Andersonarmwavinglyness, given that it's a substantive, as the grammarians say, it seems less a happening than a being, a stable substance. There's no movement to it, no verve, no change, no—

Thought: What you want is *becoming*.

World: But it's not a matter of what I want. It's simply that—

Thought: Yes, yes, alright, I know. I see. So, so how about this then? Let's say, Andersonarmwavinglynessing. A participle. That's better, no? A verbal noun. Or a noun-verb, as it were, a partner to our unity-multiplicity. And let's not even say *there is*. Let's just say the word. Nothing else. Simply, Andersonarmwavinglynessing.

Thought and world

World: Just wiggle our finger and say the word?

Thought: Maybe without the finger.

World: Or maybe without the word.

Thought: But—

World: But be that as it may, you should perhaps consider the implications of this account for us, for ourselves as source-less beings. I believe you referred to yourself as a thinking thing, even as a substance.

Thought: Yes?

World: But didn't we also agree that your account of unfree action applies to reasoning too—in which case, since it excludes the very idea of a source of action, it would seem to imply that there's no reasoner behind the reasoning.

Thought: Yes?

World: And isn't reasoning a mode of thinking?

Thought: Yes?

World: Then regarding this thinking thing you take yourself to be...

Thought: Yes, well, I suppose we'll have to conclude that there's no substance as the source of my thinking, no thinker of the thoughts.

World: And what about this 'my' then? 'My thinking,' you said.

Thought: Ha! Yes, you're right. Of course. Such talk will do for everyday communication, when there's no call for ontological precision. But to speak as accurately as possible, you're right: there can be no 'my,' nor any 'I,' no enduring substance as the subject of the deed. No deed even. There's only the happening. There's only, let's say, only the thoughtthinkinglynessing. And now that I think of it, I

125

Diamythologōmen

suppose it's better to rephrase that as thinkinglynessing, thereby effacing even the subtlest hint of a subject.

World: Even though you just said, 'now that I think of it.' Ha! But we'll overlook that 'I.'

Thought: It's so hard to avoid the tricks and traps of language!

World: It is, yes, very difficult indeed. Therefore one may be forgiven. But in any case, so now you're saying there's no you, behind yourself, as it were. Is that right?

Thought: Nor any you.

World: Nor any me, no, anyway no me behind myself.

Thought: Nor any you yourself at all, it would seem, beyond a momentary flux of, well, of nothing really— without the you behind yourself, there just isn't any you at all.

World: Nor any *you* at all then too.

Thought: Only a multiplicity of experiences distributed in space and time. No real unity of self.

World: A multiplicity distributed in—and if someone were to insist that he *feels* himself a unity?

Thought: I'd insist in turn that he no more feels himself a unity than he feels free. A feeling is one thing, correctly to conceptualize its content is another. And anyway the feeling at issue, and the subject of this feeling too, would themselves be but ephemeral experiences of some subset of the multiple distributed simple subjectivities.

World: Simple subjectivities?

Thought: Simple, yes. By which I mean no collective whole. A multiplicity of individual subjectivities that doesn't actually constitute an overarching unity.

Thought and world

World: Multiple unities but no single subsuming one? The unity-multiplicity?

Thought: That's right. Regardless whether the simples—one, some, or all of them—construct such a totalizing unity for themselves, in the playground of their imaginations.

World: The playground of their imaginations, you say?

Thought: Yes, well, it just came to me in the moment.

World: You mean it came in the moment to some simple subjectivity or subjectivities, one or some among the unity-multiplicity that doesn't really amount to you.

Thought: That's right.

World: And now here's another such simple subjectivity, in *this* moment.

Thought: That's right.

World: And another, in *this* moment.

Thought: Yes, I see your point. But look, it may be now we've found the becoming you were seeking.

World: The innocence of becoming.

Thought: Innocence, yes! Exactly! For if there's no doer behind the deed—

World: Nor any deed, you said.

Thought: Right. If there's neither doer nor deed, then nothing is responsible for being as it is.

World: Nor anyone?

Thought: Nor anyone, that's right. Nothing nor anyone responsible.

World: Nor any *being* any particular way for which to *be* responsible.

Thought: Apparently not.

World: So only the happening? Subject-less happening?

Diamythologōmen

Thought: Only the subject-less happening.
World: Object-less too, I suppose.
Thought: I suppose so, yes.
World: Including the happening that is this conversation?
Thought: Including that too, of course.
World: And your thinking?
Thought: Yes, that too.
Word: The subject-less and object-less happening which some simple subjectivities mistake for you thinking?
Thought: I...
World: Oh, and now *you're* the quiet one?
Thought: ...
World: But after all, we're only playing, right, in the playground of our imaginations?
Thought: Yes, of course, you're right. Forgive me. But I was thinking—
World: *You*, were *thinking*?
Thought: Exactly! That's the problem, isn't it? I can't say what I want to say. But anyway I'll just say it. I was thinking of your objecting to the idea that anyone or anything might *be* any particular way.
World: Yes?
Thought: Well, maybe we should drop that little word, 'be.'
World: It isn't innocent, is it?
Thought: Nor guilty either, I suppose. But it does perhaps mislead.
World: Unintentionally, of course.
Thought: Of course. I believe this follows from all that we've just said.

Thought and world

World: It does, yes. And this does too.

Thought: What does too?

World: No, not what.

Thought: Not what?

World: Exactly! Not what. Not that but this. If we drop *to be*, we'll have to drop its partners too.

Thought: Its partners?

World: Yes.

Thought: Which partners?

World: You don't know? But I thought that's what you meant yourself when earlier you proposed that we not say *there is* Andersonarmwavinglynessing, but rather simply say the word.

Thought: Oh, I see. You're referring to the *is*.

World: To the what?

Thought: To the *is*.

World: *What* is?

Thought: *That* is.

World: That is *what*? What *is* that?

Thought: No, stop! Listen. You're playing with me again. I know. And you know very well which *is* I mean.

World: 'I,' you say?

Thought: Yes, well, and 'you,' you say?! But forget all that for now. I'm trying to agree with you, or anyway with what I think you mean to say about the so-called partners of being. May I?

World: Yes, all right then. I'll play along. I'm happy to.

Thought: Thank you. So, after we've eliminated *being*, it's not only nouns and pronouns we'll have to drop, but verbs too. Anyway those that imply duration or stability—and *is* of course is the prime example.

World: It is.

Thought: But please stop playing with me now! I'm agreeing with you. I too believe this also follows from all that we've just said.

World: And what have we said, exactly?

Thought: We've said, I think—or, well, let's overlook that 'I' again, if you don't mind.

World: Of course we'll overlook it. And the 'we' and the 'you,' too. But anyway do go on.

Thought: But how to begin? How even to end? I don't know. We are source-less simple subjectivities, I want to say. Somehow. But I *don't* want to say either 'we' or 'I' or 'are' or 'am' or 'is.' Ah, the blasted limits of language!

World: Words and grammar!

Thought: So perhaps there's nothing to say but this: *Becoming*. Neither 'I am' nor 'You are' nor 'It is.' Just this single word.

World: Or—

Thought: Or better yet: sourcelesslynessing.

World: Oh, yes, another fine coinage, that! But maybe there's nothing left to say at all. Maybe there's only—

Thought: Only the finger! The wiggling of the finger!

World: The wiggling of the finger, yes. Or do you mean to say, fingerwigglinglynessing?

Thought: Ha! But no, I don't mean to say that. In fact, I think that for now I'd rather not say anything at all.

World: Don't speak, just *be*?

Thought: Ha! But no, just *think*.

Notes on Plato and Nietzsche

Tues, Jan 15

The first question of the *Phaedo* is the first sentence of the dialogue, and the first word of that sentence is the hinge on which the question turns: *autos*, the intensive adjective pronoun. Echecrates to Phaedo: *You yourself* were present for the conversation between Socrates and his friends on the last day of his life?

The first answer of the dialogue is: *autos. I myself* was there.

From the very beginning of the *Phaedo*, then—literally, from the *very first word*—the question put at issue is whether the conversation recounted in the work is a first-hand report. Echecrates is anxious to learn the facts from an eyewitness, apparently because he wants to trust that his informant's report is reliable. He will later request that Phaedo relate all that happened (*tauta dê panta*) as clearly, as manifestly, as possible (*hôs saphestata*). What's at issue here is authority, and thereby veracity.

Within the frame of the dialogue the account is first-hand. Phaedo was present for the conversation; Echecrates can rely on his report. But then Phaedo reports that Plato was *not* present for the conversation ('Plato, I think, was unwell'). A surprising turn, that, and it cues us readers to reconsider this question of veracity, but now not as between Phaedo and Echecrates, but rather as between Plato and ourselves.

Diamythologōmen

That Plato calls his authority into question like this generates something akin to dramatic irony. His absence from the conversation he purportedly reports in the dialogue has no particular relevance for Echecrates or Phaedo, but for us it resonates deeply. It subverts Plato's credibility as a source of information. And since Plato himself has manufactured this, and brought it to our attention, he has, in a sense, allied himself with us *against* his characters. He communicates with us behind their backs, as it were. The irony Plato generates here is not quite—or not only—the irony of the ancient tragedies; it's rather a variety with which we're familiar in our own day, namely, irony as detachment from the truth-claims implied by one's own statements. [On this see Rorty CIS, p. 73.] Therefore, here near the beginning of the work, Plato intimates that he doesn't believe what his Socrates says—and maybe, by implication, that we shouldn't either.

So the *Phaedo* fails, as it were, the first test put within the dialogue itself. What is wanted *within* the work is a firsthand account, yet Plato suggests that *with* the work he doesn't intend to provide this. Echecrates is none the wiser for this, but we readers understand that on this irony hangs the character of the dialogue as fact or fiction, as a *logos* or a *mythos*.

Th, Jan 17

The second question of the *Phaedo* addresses the things Socrates said before he died, and how he died. Later, Echecrates asks more specifically about Socrates' death, again employing the intensifying *autos*. He wants to know about the death *itself*—*auton ton thanaton*—and even more specifically about the things said and done (*ta lechthenta kai prachthenta*) at the death itself, which can only mean the things Socrates said and did during the minutes or moments immediately preceding his death. In this way Plato directs our attention from the beginning to the end of the dialogue.

What do we find there?

Of course we find Socrates' famous 'last words,' his request that Crito sacrifice a rooster to Asclepius. [Explain the relevant background here: Asclepius son of Apollo, god of healing, etc.] But we'll come back to his last words. For now, the broader context in which Socrates speaks includes also his *last act*, which can't be inconsequential given that Plato, by way of Echecrates' request, explicitly calls our attention to it. Let's look then at 'the things done' at Socrates' death itself.

After Socrates drinks the poison, everyone in the room breaks down, crying and wailing. Phaedo even covers his face, to hide his tears or to hide himself from the scene before him. Socrates rebukes his friends for their commotion, then, after walking around a bit, he lies down. And sometime after lying down he covers himself, presumably with a sheet, as with a death shroud. He literally has to uncover himself to address Crito. Then, after having done so, he covers himself again [this isn't noted in the text, but it's implied by the official's having to uncover him to confirm that he's dead]. And finally he moves, presumably an involuntary death-spasm (hence the passive voice, *ekinêthê*), which prompts the official to uncover him.

Diamythologōmen

Obviously, Socrates' covering, uncovering, and covering himself are the most significant of his last acts. They're certainly the most unexpected. The official had directed him to walk around and then lie down, so there's nothing unusual there. But his covering himself is strange, uncanny even. It wasn't common practice for a dying man to cover himself [I demonstrate this exhaustively in my *Plato and Nietzsche*—cite one or two examples]. In fact, the action seems to have functioned in some contexts as an initiatory act, and in Plato in particular it's connected to purification, as we'll see.

Now recall my mentioning that Phaedo covered his face, and also that the official uncovered Socrates to confirm that he was dead. Here then at the end of the dialogue we have a sudden commotion of covering and uncovering, and these acts appear in the text as two pairs of symmetrical oppositions: covering-uncovering-covering-uncovering. (Phaedo covers himself; Socrates uncovers himself, after having covered himself; the official uncovers Socrates: note that the subjects of the pairs overlap, with Socrates taking the second place in the first pair and the first place of the second pair.)

And these are just the acts noted explicitly in the text. In reality there would be: Phaedo covering and uncovering himself; Socrates covering, uncovering, then covering himself, and the official uncovering and covering Socrates (though it's possible that it was Crito who covered Socrates, after closing his mouth and eyes).

This is all very odd, and one can't help but wonder what Plato intended by stressing these strange details. Remember that he explicitly calls our attention to 'the things done' (*ta...prachthenta*) at the moment of the death itself (*auton*). That he means for us to note the oppositions of covering and uncovering is suggested by these words clustering at the end of the text. They appear nowhere else in the dialogue, but here are four instances within a single Stephanus page, the final three just words part, the second and third literally back to front: Socrates uncovered himself, for he had covered himself (*ekkalupsamenos enekekalupto*). [Read aloud the relevant excerpts of the text, in the Greek—the rhythm of the two words describing Socrates is striking.]

Earlier I mentioned covering in the context of initiation. As Mary recently called to my attention, the Lovatelli urn in the *Museo Nazionale Romano* depicts Herakles being initiated into the Lesser Eleusinian Mysteries by way of a purificatory act which involves his being covered with a veil. And this of course recalls Demeter, who while mourning for her lost daughter, Persephone, sat with her head veiled before the two were reunited, in celebration of which she founded the Greater Mysteries. [Other relevant examples in PN.] But more directly related to the *Phaedo* is the *Phaedrus*, in which Socrates covers his head before delivering his first speech, and then uncovers himself before delivering his second speech explicitly as an act of purification.

Initiates of the Mysteries sought to secure for themselves a blessed afterlife, which is the subject of much of Socrates' second speech in the *Phaedrus*, and which also is, of course, a major theme of the *Phaedo*. Should we therefore conclude that Socrates' last act was aimed at a purificatory initiation? If so, an initiation into what exactly? I must confess that in the end I don't know. It's a riddle every bit as enigmatic as

Socrates' last words and—and of this I'm convinced—bound up with them.

Tues, Jan 22

Consider Socrates' first words of substance on the morning of his death. [I mean to exclude his asking Crito to see to the departure of his wife and children.] The chains have just been removed from his legs, and as he rubs his thighs he formulates a *mythos* about 'what men call' pleasure and its 'apparent opposite,' pain. One can't have one without the other following after, he says. And if Aesop had noticed this, he might have composed a '*mython*' about a god's being unable to reconcile these warring opposites and so joining them at the head.

So Aesop, *mythoi*, and apparent oppositions are on Socrates' mind first thing in the morning. And his naming Aesop prompts Cebes to inquire about his composing poems in prison. Socrates explains that a dream had often come to him throughout his life urging him to 'practice *mousikê*.' He had always thought the dream was encouraging him to continue practicing philosophy, the supreme form of *mousikê*. But now as he confronts the end of his life, he thought it best to consider whether the dream intended him to practice the popular art of poetry.

But Socrates was not a poet. He had to borrow themes from Aesop because, as a philosopher, he deals with *logoi*, not, like the poets, with *mythoi*. He is not a *mythologikos*, he says. [NB: this word is formed by the pairing of apparent opposites.]

Notes on Plato and Nietzsche

Socrates not a *mythologikos*?! But he began his morning with a *mythos*! His first thoughts on his last day were bound up with *mythoi*! And as we'll see, he blurs the apparent distinction between *logos* and *mythos* throughout the ensuing conversation, and at key moments too. At 61e, for instance, he suggests it's fitting to *mythologein* about his upcoming journey to the underworld. And this just moments after claiming he's not a *mythologikos*! And in fact he says here that it's fitting to *mythologein* until sunset, which incorporates the entire conversation into the scope of this verb, not just some small segment of it. More, at 70b he introduces his three main 'proofs' that the soul is immortal, ostensibly the central *logos* of the dialogue, by suggesting that they *diamythologômen* the matter. Later, at 110b, he calls his account of the true surface of the earth a *mythos*, and he concludes the conversation by referring to the whole thing as a *mythos* (114d).

So. Socrates, as a character in the dialogue, claims he's not a *mythologikos*. But Plato as the author makes him contradict himself. With his own words. This cannot be accidental. In fact I suspect it's another way for Plato to distance himself ironically from his central character. And let me just say this about that: in the gap (I resist writing *abyss*) between Plato's Socrates and Plato himself we just might discover, at a level deeper than Socrates' arguments for Platonic dogma, insight into Plato's thinking-life.

Th, Jan 24

Now into the *Phaedo*'s matrix of meaning and allusion comes Nietzsche, with his several accounts of *the dying Socrates* [in

BT, GS, TI: we'll consider the latter two works later]. In *The Birth of Tragedy* Socrates is the original instance and paradigm of the *theoretical man*, the master of optimistic dialectic, which we may sum up in the proposition that through the proper use of reason we can understand being and correct existence. The world is comprehensible in full, and the pains of human embodied life can be healed. The healing drug is called *reason*, its effect on the sickly organism is summed up in the word *virtue*, and the consequent spiritual state of well-being is *happiness*. In a formula, reason equals virtue equals happiness, as Nietzsche puts it in *Twilight of the Idols*. Through reason one can know virtue; he who knows virtue will be virtuous; the virtuous are happy. Hence the imperturbable calm with which Socrates confronts his death, provokes it even (through his conduct at trial—the Athenians would have preferred to exile him). His knowledge has liberated him from the fear of death.

As a young man Plato aspired to be a tragedian, but he was so enraptured by the image of the dying Socrates that he burned his tragic poems and dedicated himself to the Socratic way of life. [I'm still paraphrasing N here.] But his natural artistic impulse was too vigorous simply to dissipate. It welled up and expressed itself in a new form of poetry, which combined narrative, lyric, and drama, poetry and prose, a precursor in a sense to the novel.

Here it's worth pausing to observe that Plato's copious output of writing marks a significant departure from the Socratic way of life, given that Socrates famously wrote nothing—nothing anyway besides the Aesopian verses and the hymn to Apollo he composed in prison (to assume for now the veracity of this detail). Socrates was a public talker; Plato was a private writer.

But be this as it may, Nietzsche's not impressed. He insists that as a writer Plato *subordinates* poetry to prose; the *mythos* in his work is a mere *ancilla* to the *logos*, art a handmaid to science. In this way tragedy finally died—Plato drove through the heart of tragedy the dagger of reason which Socrates had forged—and the tragic worldview yielded to the therapeutic. And this anti-tragic, anti-Greek, rational-scientific perspective eventually overspread the west like a virus (exploiting Christianity as a carrier for a time).

But Nietzsche points to Socrates' dream ('practice *mousikê*') as an indication that Socrates had his doubts about 'the limits of logic.' And in this context he introduces the type of the 'musical Socrates,' the man who pursues science to the point at which it bites its own tail—presumably in the Kantian-Schopenhauerian insight that science cannot fathom the depths of nature, but can only track the causal relationships that operate within, and *as*, the representation, the *phaenomena*. [Elaborate: Later Nietzsche rejects the details of Schopenhauer's idealism, but he continues to insist that scientific knowledge of causes does not grasp unadulterated truth. This is his so-called falsificationism. The scientist's belief in truth is the last remnant of the ascetic ideal, as fully as metaphysical and misguided as the Christian's belief in God (we'll go into all this in detail if we have time for the 'Third Essay' of the *Genealogy* later in the semester).] In any case, the musical Socrates is the man who pursues science to the point of its dead end, who then realizes that art is the 'necessary correlative of, and supplement for, science.' This is the return of the tragic insight: science cannot after all know and correct being.

Science in the end turns into art, Nietzsche says. The regeneration of art and myth is somehow the teleological necessity of science. More, religion and science are themselves manifestations of art, poetry, myth. Science is art which temporarily—perhaps even for millennia—mistakes itself for something else.

It is standard to claim that with his expression 'the Socrates who practices music' Nietzsche intends to allude to himself. This may well be right. And if he did intend this, I for one would agree with him. But I would add that *Plato* is the *original of this type*. The surface of Nietzsche's *Birth of Tragedy* suggests that he would disagree, and maybe he would—*if* he's serious that Plato subordinated poetry to prose, art to science as dialectic. But does he really mean this? In *Beyond Good and Evil* he writes that Plato was 'too noble' for Socratism. Plato *used* Socrates, as an 'audacious interpreter' picks up a popular tune to 'vary it into the infinite and impossible—namely, into all of his own masks and multiplicities.'

So Socrates is a mask behind which Plato hides—though he reveals himself simultaneously through the masterful variations he plays on Socrates' original tune. And here I think of the striking stretch in BT 15 where, specifically in the context of discussing *the dying Socrates*, while contrasting Socrates as the theoretical man with the artist, Nietzsche deploys a barrage of words for covering and uncovering. The man of science is fascinated with the act of uncovering

(*Enthüllung*), and with studying every discarded cover (*Hülle*), whereas the artist is enraptured by the cover (*Hülle*) that always remains, even after every successful act of uncovering (*Enthüllung*). And this recalls a similar flurry of these same words in GS 339, which includes the claim that the highest summit of good things remains concealed and covered (*Verhülltes*) for most observers, even for the best of us, and that that which does uncover (*enthüllt*) itself for us, uncovers (*enthüllt*) itself only once—precisely as Socrates uncovered himself one time only at the end of his life. This section by the way immediately precedes Nietzsche's second discussion of *the dying Socrates*, in which he refers to Socrates' last words as *verhüllten*—disguised, masked, literally, covered.

All this is to suggest that Nietzsche, unlike the many scholars who have scrutinized Socrates' last words, was struck—as I too am struck—by the interplay of the *Phaedo*'s final covering-uncovering oppositions. For him it serves as an image of the differences between the artist and the man of science. He doesn't speculate as to its meaning for Plato.

But what should *we* make of it? Does Plato mean somehow to reveal himself behind the mask of Socrates? The artist behind the aspiring knower? Is he finally lowering the veil, killing Socrates that he himself may live? In short, was *Plato* really the dreamer of Socrates' dream?

'Plato, don't confine yourself to Socratic rationalism, to the *logos* as opposed to *mythos*. These are only apparent opposites, and *logos* is a mode of *mythos*. Plato, Plato! Wake up! Wake up and be a poet-philosopher! Practice *mousikê*!'

Diamythologōmen

If Plato did dream such a dream, the fact would account for the anti-Socratic, poetic elements that infuse the best of his dialogues, the *Phaedo* for example. And it strikes me that the shadow of doubt cast over the dialogue's historicity by the frame conversation ['Plato, I think, was unwell'], and the repeated stress on *mythos* throughout—it strikes me that all this suggests that Plato may well have been the dreamer. If he wasn't, then I want to say at least that he interpreted Socrates' dream much differently than the dreamer did himself. The historical Socrates may have privileged *logoi* over *mythoi*, reason over creativity, but the Socrates of the *Phaedo*—which we suspect from the beginning of the work may be more Plato than Socrates—is a *mythologikos*, despite his protestation to the contrary. [Nietzsche also toyed with the idea that Plato's Socrates is more Plato than Socrates, as when he described him as 'Plato in front, Plato behind, and in the middle Chimera,' (BGE 190, alluding to *Iliad* 6.181).]

Let's sum up the spirit of the *Phaedo* this way: in and through the dialogue Plato turns Socrates against himself, turns him into his opposite, from the theoretical man into the artist—into himself, Plato. If this is right, then, as I said, *Plato is the musical Socrates*. And why not? It was Plato after all who erected a shrine to the Muses on the grounds of the Academy.

Tues, Jan 29

When Simmias and Cebes call on Socrates to account for his not resenting (*aganaktein*) dying, Socrates replies at length with what he terms a 'defense.' He hopes it will prove more successful than his defense before the jurors at trial. I suppose success depends in this case on one's expectations. If a defense should provide more than a mere description of the defendant's peculiar perspective and psychology, if it should demonstrate the soundness of the assumptions that motivate his actions, then Socrates fails miserably. For his long defense amounts to little more than an analogy between the figurative separation (*apallagê*) of soul from body in the life and activities of the philosopher and the literal separation of soul from body at death.

Supposedly literal, I should say, since the claim that death is the separation of soul from body is merely stipulated, at 64c. [This is significant—as we'll see, Socrates relies throughout his discussion on the assumption that the soul is a substance in its own right independent of the body—which is not a minor detail to assume without argument!] The idea is that since Socrates thinks of philosophy as involving a sort of separation, and since death is separation, then it would be ridiculous (*geloion*) for him to resent the literal condition that he had been figuratively enacting as a philosopher. But of course the analogy is pertinent only if the figurative and literal forms of separation are relevantly similar. They're not.

The first of the three figurative instances of separation that Socrates relates—the philosopher's disdain and disregard for bodily pleasures and ornamentations (64c-65a)—is nothing like the literal separation of death; it is merely the fact that philosophers care little about their corporeal selves, that they tend toward asceticism.

The second instance of figurative separation involves the mode of the philosopher's approach to knowledge of the

Forms (65a-67b). Since truth is not accessible through the senses—even the poets insist on this—the soul in seeking the truth relies on itself alone (*autê kath' autên*), disregarding the deliverances of the senses, which tend only to confuse or mislead it. (Socrates calls this independence of the intellect from sensation 'purification,' which he associates with separation at 67a-d.) But this amounts to nothing more than the affirmation that conceptual reasoning is superior to empirical observation. And even if we grant that the senses play no role whatever in the acquisition of knowledge (and ignoring for now that this is inconsistent with the account at 74a-75c), this is still a thoroughly figurative sense of separation. Besides, the boldest claim that Socrates is entitled to derive from all this, as he himself admits, is that *either* knowledge is not possible at all, *or* it is possible only after death. Well, a skeptic might reply, perhaps knowledge isn't possible after all.

The third figurative instance of separation—regarding the philosopher's approach to virtue (68c-69c)—also bears no resemblance to death; it's the fact that philosophers ground virtue on wisdom (*phronêsis*) rather than on considerations of pleasure and pain. Following this claim, and by way of appeal to the Mysteries, Socrates likens the virtues to modes of purification (*katharmos*, 69b-d), which, as I just noted, he identifies with separation. But, again, this is separation as it is possible while alive—in a word, figurative separation.

And why, by the way, does Socrates say that those who founded the Mysteries were likely *speaking in riddles* when they said that the purified souls of the dead will dwell with the gods (69c-d)—when this is precisely the claim that he himself has made about the soul (63b-c)? Is his own talk of purification, separation, and the soul after death dwelling with the gods a mystifying riddle? Does he not really mean it? Does Plato not?

Throughout his defense Socrates expresses hope that his soul will live after the death of his body. He says, for example, that he has good hope (*euelpis*) that something good awaits good men after death (63c), also that he has much hope (*pollê elpis*, 67b), and good hope (*meta agathês elpidos*, 67c), that he'll acquire knowledge after death. But Socrates' hopes are no substitute for arguments.

In the end, then, and to repeat: Socrates' defense comes down to this: 'Well, it would be ridiculous for someone who thinks of philosophy as I do to resent dying.' [Really, just compare 67d12-e2 to my paraphrase.]

For Socrates' defense to amount to more than an explanation of his own idiosyncratic motivation for not resenting death, it would have to demonstrate, first, that the soul really separates from the body at death, and, second, that this literal separation is relevantly similar to the living philosopher's figurative separation. Cebes recognizes at least the need to justify the first point, which motivates his request that Socrates prove—or at least persuade his interlocutors—that the soul doesn't just dissolve and blow away at death. If Socrates could convince them of this, he says, there would be much good hope (*pollê...elpis...kai kalê*) that the things he has said by way of his defense are true. Not confidence, mind you, just hope.

Diamythologōmen

Th, Jan 31

That Nietzsche ends *The Gay Science* with reference to Socrates, and in particular with a staged confrontation between Socrates and Zarathustra on the field of their relation to the value of life, suggests a lens through which to read the first section of the book, on *the teachers of the purpose of existence*. The Persian Zoroaster would be one such teacher, Buddha and Jesus would be others. But in this connection Nietzsche often had Socrates in mind, especially the dying Socrates of the *Phaedo*.

The surface message of the *Phaedo* is that there is another world, another life, behind or beneath this world and life. Thus the dialogue precisely satisfies Nietzsche's description of an 'anti-natural' system founded on 'a second, different existence' which 'unhinges by means of [its] new mechanics the old, ordinary existence.' And in the *Phaedo* as in Nietzsche's account, this second world is depicted as first, as ontologically prior to the world of our experience, more valuable too. In this otherworld—this *Hinterwelt*—and indeed because of it, our present lives have meaning, purpose, and consequence. The eternal fate of our immortal souls is at stake. Thus Socrates says he was motivated to leave nothing undone in life, so far as he was able, but was eager in every way to make it to this otherworld after death with a pure soul (69c-d). This is serious; life is serious; philosophy as a way of life, as a purification, is serious indeed. As Nietzsche says, the 'ethical teacher' (read Socrates), the 'teacher of the purpose of existence,' strives to ensure that 'we do not *laugh* at existence…or at him.'

Simmias laughs at Socrates when he suggests that those who engage in philosophy properly (*orthôs*) practice nothing else but dying and being dead. His laughter in fact is stressed by three instances of *gelaô* in one sentence. In response to Simmias's laughter Socrates introduces the analogy on which his defense depends, namely the separation of soul from body in death and in the life of the philosopher, which we discussed on Tuesday. And when he concludes his defense, Simmias is silent. Presumably he now realizes the seriousness of our situation. The gods are watching.

Nietzsche foresees a day when we have deflated the solemn pretensions of *Phaedo*-Platonism, and every similar metaphysical-moral mode of seriousness, when we have finally realized that all that happens happens 'necessarily and always, spontaneously and without any purpose.' On that day we shall realize also that the species is all, the individual nothing. We shall comprehend the innocence of becoming. And the laughter welling up from these liberating insights will form an alliance with wisdom to produce *la gaya scienza*. The individual is not a center around which the cosmos revolves, his fate a focus of eternal judgement and consequence. The one is zero, innocent and unserious. In this case laughter is permitted, encouraged even. Laughter as a symptom of the great health.

Tues, Feb 5

In reply to Socrates' defense of his not resenting death, Cebes remarks that there's much mistrust (*pollên apistian*) among men about such talk regarding the soul as Socrates' claim that at death it separates from the body. Perhaps this

Diamythologōmen

explains the fact—to which Socrates alludes at 70b-c—that the comic poets so delighted in provoking laughter at his prattling on about such matters, about things in the heavens and under the earth, the very subject of his *mythos-logos* in the *Phaedo*. In any case, Socrates replies to Cebes' concern with what we might call a defense of his defense. This consists of three arguments for the immortality of the soul, the first of which is the so-called argument from opposites.

It's at this point, by the way, as I noted a week or so ago, that Socrates asks whether they should *diamythologômen* (literally, 'mythologize about') these matters, specifically about whether the soul exists somewhere after death and possesses some power (*dunamis*) and intelligence (*phronêsis*).

The argument from opposites is inspired by a *palaios logos*, an ancient story, 'which we remember,' which presumably Socrates believes, and which if true justifies his expectation of life after death. According to this ancient *logos*, souls exist in the underworld, arriving there from here, and then they arrive back here again, coming to be from those who have died. If this is so, Socrates says, then our souls must exist in the underworld after death, which presumably implies that souls do indeed separate from bodies at death—if, that is, we should trust an ancient *logos* that amounts to nothing more than a pious old Pythagorean *mythos*.

The argument is simple, or at least it begins that way. All things which have opposites come to be from their opposites, the weaker from the stronger, for example, or the worse from the better. This makes perfect sense, of course, but when Socrates switches from comparative predicates to states of being, one wonders whether the move is legitimate, truth-preserving, as the logicians say. The states of waking and sleeping, Socrates' first example of opposite states, do indeed come to be from each other, if not as obviously, and not in the same way as, the lesser degree of some variable property comes to be from a greater degree of it, and vice versa. But what about the states of living and being dead? Is each of these really the state of some existing thing? None of Socrates' other examples imply the non-existence of the bearer of the comparative predicate, or the thing in the state. A weaker man exists no less than a stronger man, a sleeping man no less than one awake. But does a dead man exist no less than a living man?

If we take the soul as the subject of these states, as 'alive' when joined with a body and 'dead' when separated from it (in accord with Socrates' stipulated definition of death), then, yes, there would indeed be a subject of the state *being dead*, namely the still existing soul. But to take Socrates' point this way would be to grant him here, as a premise of his argument, the very conclusion the argument is supposed to establish. In short, one wonders whether Socrates' talk of living and being dead as states doesn't beg the question. *Is* there a thing (the soul) which is the subject of the state *being dead* (but yet exists)? That's the question at issue.

Th, Feb 7

Today's section of the *Phaedo* provides a detailed account of the doctrine that learning is recollection. Supplemented with the parallel section in the *Meno* (to which Cebes probably refers at 73a-b), it's as thorough an account as one will find of most any doctrine in the dialogues. But is there an argument here for the immortality of the soul? There is not. As Socrates himself remarks at the conclusion of this section (76d-e), if the Forms exist, the soul must be immortal. If they don't exist, then the *logos* he's provided has been spoken in vain (*allôs ... eirêmenos*). But he doesn't even attempt to prove the relevant antecedent. Everyone he's speaking with simply assumes the existence of 'these realities,' the Forms. Moreover, Socrates hasn't quite stated the conditional correctly. It isn't true that there's an 'equal necessity' that the Forms exist and that our souls exist before birth. There could well be Forms but no soul. One must assume, not just Forms, but the doctrine that learning is recollection. The doctrine, if true, would necessitate both the Forms and pre-existent souls. But nothing in the *Phaedo* proves any of this.

What should we make of the total absence of an argument here? Has Plato compelled his Socrates to admit the groundlessness of his belief in Forms to cast doubt on the relevant metaphysics, and thereby also the immortality of the soul? Later, as we'll see, he appeals again to Forms to justify belief in an immortal soul, but there too he simply, and quite explicitly, hypothesizes Forms, with no argument whatever. It must be relevant that Plato doesn't just provide the semblance of arguments, but also makes a point of employing his characters to imply or state outright that the apparent proofs are insufficient or incomplete.

And as for the so-called affinity argument—the third of Socrates' 'proofs' of the immortality of the soul—it's not even really an argument. It's a charm sung to soothe childish fears (77d-78a). And another analogy. And proceeding again on the assumption that immaterial souls exist. The bald assumption: 'The soul, as we conceive it, is immaterial, like the Forms. And therefore like the Forms it has no parts. But that which is non-composite cannot be dissolved. Therefore the soul is altogether indissoluble, which is to say immortal.' This is my paraphrase, but the 'as we conceive it' faithfully depicts the fact that Socrates assumes not only the existence of the soul but specific details about its nature to conclude that it's immortal.

Actually, Socrates concludes that the soul is altogether indissoluble, 'or something close to this' (*hê engus ti toutou*, 80b10). A surprising qualification. So the soul is only *mostly* indissoluble? Most of the soul but not all of it? Or for most of time but not forever? Or, what? Is this an indirect admission that the argument doesn't amount to a proof—which would at least be honest since it's hardly even an argument. A chain of inferences, no doubt; but not a proof. Rather an elaboration of the implications of various dubious hypotheses.

Tues, Feb 12

More notable than the three so-called arguments considered so far is the introduction in the section following the affinity argument of the theme of reincarnation and several formulations that are generally taken to imply the possibility of a permanent escape from the cycle of rebirth. But despite near universal scholarly agreement, the consensus on this point is mistaken: the *Phaedo* does *not* teach escape from the cycle of rebirth. It's true that nothing in the text explicitly rules it out—but why would it? The idea never even comes up, so there's no call to argue against it. Moreover, nothing said in the text implies it, much less states it outright. The doctrine simply isn't there. There's just no definitive—nor even any *nearly* definitive—evidence for it in the text.

This is central to our exploration of the *Phaedo*, and indeed of Plato's intentions as an author, a philosophical author. It's pertinent also to an evaluation of Nietzsche's reading of the *Phaedo*. So, although it requires inspecting many details at length, I gather here in one place each and every one of the relevant passages.

The *locus classicus* is 114c, at the conclusion of Socrates' description of the underworld and the afterlife, and just prior to his drinking of the hemlock. [I'm jumping ahead now to the end of the work, to cover the most important passage first. Later I'll back up to examine the others in the order they appear in the text.] Socrates says that 'those who have purified themselves sufficiently by way of philosophy live without bodies in the future, and they come to dwellings still more beautiful that these [discussed previously in the myth], which it's not easy to describe, nor is there sufficient time at present [to do so]' (114c2-6).

Does this passage imply the possibility of full and final escape from the body? It's not clear that it does, not unless one is specifically searching the text for the doctrine.

Socrates says that those who have been sufficiently purified by philosophy will live without a body in the future, *eis ton epeita chronon*. But there's nothing in this expression that necessitates that we take it to mean *eternally*. It may suggest only that the soul after death will live without a body throughout the ensuing postmortem state, until it's reborn. The expression *ho epeita chronos* appears elsewhere in Plato, but nowhere does it unambiguously indicate literal eternity: At Phdr 244e, Symp 208e, and Tim 90d the meaning is ambiguous between 'in the future' and 'eternally'; at Rep 357b, Phdr 240e and 257d, Symp 200d (x3), Menex 241c-d, and Leg 656e, 688d, 704a, 741c, and 754d it definitely does *not* mean 'eternally.'

But maybe there's a way to defend the reading of 'eternally' here. The *eis ton epeita chronon* is immediately preceded by *to parapan* (altogether, absolutely), so if we take the two together then we might have reason to read the whole as 'altogether in future time,' or 'in eternity.' But in context it's ambiguous whether *to parapan* modifies *eis ton epeita chronon* or the preceding claim that after death souls will live without a body, *aneu...sômatôn zôsi*. If the latter is the correct reading, then Socrates' claim is that the soul of the purified philosopher will live after death *altogether without a body*.

How then should we take the *to parapan*, as modifying the temporal clause or the bodiless clause? Plato doesn't modify any such temporal expression with *to parapan* anywhere in the early or middle dialogues. Surely this must weaken the case for this reading—especially since he *does* elsewhere employ the expression in a manner consistent with the use we're considering here, placement after a verb to modify a predicate preceding the verb. There's an example even in the *Phaedo* (at 89e2-3). Therefore, we can be certain that *aneu...sômatôn zôsi to parapan* is a perfectly grammatical, natural, and even Platonic, reading.

That the expression is not only grammatical but sensible, and even consistent with the substance of the dialogue, is evident given that earlier (at 81c and 83d) Socrates speaks of the impure soul as being mixed up with corporeality (*dieilêmmenên...hupo tou sômatoeidous*), earthy (*geôdes*), corporeal (*sômatoeidê*), and quite full of (or infected with: *anaplea*) the body. Read against this background, Socrates at 114c would be stressing that the thoroughly purified soul will depart from the body at death taking no corporeal admixture with it. In short, that it will live in the future *altogether without a body*. But, again, the future at issue may well be finite, enduring only until the soul's rebirth into another body. [I omitted the 'altogether' from my translation of the passage above so as not to imply one or the other reading.]

As for the other passages that may be taken to imply escape from the cycle of rebirth, they are all more ambiguous than 114c. Let's consider them in order.

In the course of his 'defense,' when discussing purification as involving separation (*to chôrizein*) of soul from body, Socrates refers to the soul's gathering itself together with itself (*autên kath' autên*) and, having been released (*ekluomenên*) from the bonds of the body, dwelling (*oikein*) alone with itself in the future (67c-d). This is the first passage in the text that a reader in search of the doctrine of permanent escape might identify as implying it. In itself, however, it isn't at all obvious that this is the point. The soul dwells alone in the future—this could imply any number of facts about the state of the soul in the underworld prior to its rebirth. It certainly doesn't demand to be read as implying an eternal future.

As to eternity, we can massage the passage by associating it with 114c as follows: when Socrates says that the soul can live separately from the body not just now (*en tôi nun paronti*) but in the future (*en tôi epeita* [*chronôi*]), we may urge that this prefigures the *eis ton epeita chronon* at 114c, and also that the *oikein* ('to dwell') prefigures the *oikêseis* ('dwellings') at 114c. But this requires that we read quite a bit of extra material into the passage as it stands, and besides, since the passage at 114c is itself ambiguous, it won't serve to disambiguate any other passage.

The second passage one might take as suggesting the possibility of permanent escape from the cycle of rebirth appears at 69c where, at the conclusion of his defense, Socrates says that he has confidence that after death he will 'dwell with the gods' (*meta theôn oikêsei*). But that's it; that's all it says. Obviously, one has to read much into this passage to derive permanent escape from it. One could, for example, associate the *oikêsei* with the *oikêseis* at 114c, but this is a weaker association even than the previous example, which at least made reference to 'the future.' Besides, Socrates says that this way of describing the postmortem fate of the soul is a riddling way of putting the matter, as in the Mysteries. So who really knows what he has in mind here?

We hear nothing else of anything like the possibility of escape from the cycle of rebirth until after the affinity argument. Then Socrates says that the soul that has practiced philosophy properly, as training for death, will go away to that which is of the same kind (*to homoion*)—divine, deathless, and wise—and, arriving there (*aphikomenêi*) and escaping human ills (*kakôn tôn anthrôpeiôn apêllagmenêi*), it will live in the future with the gods (*ton loipon chronon meta theôn diagousa*) (81a). As in the previous example, Socrates here refers to this way of putting the matter as relating to the Mysteries, which is to say, presumably, it's a riddling formulation. And anyway there's nothing in the passage to necessitate that his reference to the future implies eternity. The expression *ho loipos chronos* may be taken to mean 'eternally' at Ap 41c, but it most definitely does *not* mean this at *Meno* 81b (quoting Pindar), Rep 460a, Menex 246b, or Leg 840d, 929e, or 954d.

Immediately following this passage here at 81a, Socrates discusses reincarnation into animals, including the human animal, and in this connection he says that no one but the absolutely purified philosopher may approach or attain the race of the gods (*eis...theôn genos...aphikneisthai*) (82b-c). Now, one might argue that since Socrates mentions reincarnation into the human form here, he means to imply that the purified philosopher will not even be subject to later embodiment as a human. But his point in this passage is not about the human in general, but rather about a particular type of human—moderate souls will be reincarnated as moderate humans. Nothing in the passage suggests that this exhausts the possibilities of re-embodiment as a human. Moreover, given that this formulation shares with those at 69c and 81a talk of being with the gods, it might well be yet another riddling articulation of the matter as promulgated in the Mysteries [in fact it's *probable* that it is, because this passage is more or less continuous with the 81a passage].

The images of imprisonment and liberation following this section on reincarnation—especially Socrates' saying at 84a2-5 that the soul of the philosopher would not think that after philosophy has freed it, it should give itself over to pleasures and pains and thereby 'bind itself fast again' (*heautên palin au egkatadein*)—these images might suggest to a careless reader that the properly purified soul can avoid being bound fast again in a new life after its liberation from the body at death. But in fact the liberation and imprisonment at issue here (from 82d through 84b) are all of the figurative variety we discussed a couple of weeks ago. The 'liberation' is the living soul's 'separation' from the body in its search for knowledge, which is to say the living philosopher's exercise of reason without relying on the senses. Imprisonment is soul's believing that truth is what the body (i.e., the senses) says it is (as at 83d6). Moreover, at the conclusion of this section Socrates insists, not that the soul of the philosopher who lives rightly will escape the body never to be reborn, but only that it will not scatter in the wind and dissolve.

In the middle of this section on imprisonment and liberation Socrates contends [or seems to contend—I'll explain the 'seems to' shortly] that the soul's being reincarnated (*palin piptein eis allo sôma*: lit, to fall back into another body) is the greatest and most extreme of all bad things (*pantôn megiston te kakôn kai eschaton*, 83c2-3), the problem being that the re-embodied soul has no share in intercourse with the divine, pure, and single-formed (83e-84a). This section concludes with mention of the pure soul after death approaching or attaining (*eis...aphikomenê*) that which is akin (*to suggenes*) to the true and divine (*to alêthes kai to theion*) after having escaped from human ills (*apêllachthai tôn anthrôpinôn kakôn*) (84b). If reincarnation is the worst thing possible, then unless we humans are condemned to suffering terribly forever, there must be some way to escape the cycle.

So it might seem—if, that is, we haven't read the relevant passage carefully. Notice that it's not reincarnation in and of itself that Socrates identifies as the terrible thing at issue, with the negative implication that those who avoid this terrible thing are never reincarnated. The terrible thing is rather being reincarnated *quickly* (**tachu** *palin piptein eis allo sôma*, 83d10-e1), without the opportunity to spend time among the divine. [Cebes affirms this point with the superlative response formula *alêthestata...legeis* (83e4), one of only three instances of his using this formula in the work.] Why this is terrible is evident when we consider it together with the immediately preceding section on reincarnation into different kinds of animals. The problem is that the all-too-quickly reincarnated soul will fail to acquire the knowledge (through commune with the Forms) sufficient to ensure a desirable future incarnation.

That quick reincarnation, rather than reincarnation in itself, is really what's at issue here is supported by the *Phaedrus* [if we may interpret one dialogue by way of another, which is not uncontroversial]. In the *Phaedrus* some souls after death have no view of the truth beyond the rim of heaven; they are 'uninitiated' (*ateleis*, 248b4), and they do not spend time with the gods (248c). This is reminiscent of the description in the *Phaedo* of those who die unpurified and so do not dwell with the gods as 'uninitiated' (*atelestos*, 69c5). And in the *Phaedrus* even those souls that do accompany a god and see something of the truth, souls that are described as initiates (249c6-8)—*even these souls are reincarnated* (249a-b), even they become heavy (*barunthêi*, *baruntheisa*: 248c) and fall (*pesêi*: 248c, *pesousai*: 250a) to earth, precisely as the 'earthy' souls in the *Phaedo* are heavy (*baru*, *barunetai*: 81c) and not long (*tachu*) after death fall (*piptein*: 83d) into another bodily incarnation. Therefore, if we may appeal to the *Phaedrus* for assistance interpreting the scheme of reincarnation in the *Phaedo*, we may equate the souls in the former work who fail to attend a god and so see nothing of the truth with those in the latter who are reincarnated quickly and so have no intercourse with the gods. And, more significantly, we may equate those souls in the *Phaedrus* who, despite being initiates who keep company with the gods, nevertheless eventually become heavy and fall to earth to be reincarnated, with those in the *Phaedo* who practice philosophy correctly but who, we may infer, are not permanently released from the cycle of rebirth but are eventually reborn.

So, there we have every passage in the *Phaedo* into which one might read the doctrine of permanent escape from the cycle of rebirth. These accounts share a common vocabulary of *escape from the body* and from *human ills* and of *arrival* in the realm of *the gods* or *the divine*, to which the *purified soul* is *akin* and where it will *live in the future*. But does all this amount to escape from the cycle of rebirth? It's not obvious that it does. Not at all.

If Plato means to affirm the possibility of a final and permanent escape from the cycle of rebirth, one wonders why he nowhere indicates this explicitly. We have just examined every passage that may be taken to imply it, but in none is the idea stressed or even stated unambiguously. Socrates never isolates, identifies, emphasizes, and explains the idea in full. Nor do his interlocutors enquire about it; they seek no clarification, expansion, or proof of it. It's as if to them it isn't even implied. There's certainly no reason to believe that no one mentions it explicitly because everyone simply takes it for granted, as obvious. Escape from the cycle of rebirth was not a standard teaching, not in general at the time nor in Plato's dialogues. If Plato meant to teach it, then, one would expect something more to be made of it. That nothing much is made of it—and that *nothing at all* is made of it without deep (I might even say *fatal*) ambiguities—this makes me suspect that it isn't really there.

[Radcliffe Edmonds is dubious of the idea that any Greek of Plato's day conceived the possibility of escape from the cycle of rebirth. See his *Myths of the Underworld Journey*, also the chapter 'Life in the afterlife' of his *Redefining Ancient Orphism*.]

Th, Feb 14

The bulk of the *Phaedo* we've covered so far is Socrates' defense of his defense for not resenting dying by way of demonstrating that something good happens to good men at death. Or, if not quite demonstrating, then providing good hope of this. Socrates can't really claim to have demonstrated anything at this point because each of his three arguments simply assumes the existence of the soul as a separate, or separable, substance that escapes the body at death and which gathers itself together with itself. Socrates helps himself to this account from his stipulated definition of death (at 64c), which includes escape (*apallagê*), separation (*chôris*), and the soul's being gathered together with itself (*autên kath' autên*). Even Cebes, whose doubts about the soul's continued existence after death motivate Socrates' three arguments, assumes that the soul escapes the body at death (*apallagêi tou sômatos*, 70a2); he wonders only whether it does in fact gather itself together with itself (*autê kath' autên sunêthroismenê*), exist somewhere, and have 'some power and intelligence' (70a-b).

Perhaps the lack of substantive argumentation—to say nothing of *proof*—explains Socrates' admission following the affinity argument that his reasoning throughout the dialogue so far is insufficient. There remain, he says, many suspicions and vulnerable points (*pollas...hupopsias kai antilabas*) in what has been said (84c); and he invites Simmias and Cebes, who are evidently still puzzled (*aporeiton*, the verb is cognate with *aporia*), to indicate anything that seems to them to have been said inadequately (*endeôs*). And although this admission follows most closely on the affinity argument, we may take it to apply to each of the three previous arguments, since Socrates' conclusion (at 84b) that one need not fear that upon separation the soul will fly off and go away and be nothing anywhere any longer is an almost word for word repetition of the terms employed by Cebes

Diamythologōmen

when (at 70a) he objected to Socrates' defense on the grounds that men doubt whether the soul exists after death, which prompted Socrates to offer his three arguments. In short, here (at 84b) ends (the first phase of) Socrates' defense of his defense, begun way back at 70b, and upon concluding he acknowledges that his arguments are still radically insufficient (I take the 'radically' from his admitting to 'many' vulnerabilities).

Tues, Feb 19

In GS 110 Nietzsche writes of what he calls 'life-preserving errors,' the errors of 'things, substances, bodies,' for example. In a word, the error of *being*. Passed down through the gene pool, and also by way of education, these errors are 'incorporated' into the organism, integrated into the perceptual and cognitive systems of the human animal, whereby eventually they come to constitute 'knowledge' and, as an assemblage of natural inclinations and intellectual assumptions, they function as the standard for establishing knowledge in the future. They regulate our experience of the real, determine what counts as a fact. In short, they disclose the world to us—but *it's a world of their construction*. It's a *fabricated reality*. Thus our truths are grounded on, literally constituted by, fictions.

These errors are at work in Platonism (not to say in Plato), especially in the naive trust in, first, the deliverances of the senses (despite the constant railing against the senses as unreliable and immoral—I'll come back to this), and, second, the concept-formation and reasoning powers of the brain. From this trust grow the 'erroneous articles of faith' (in *being*, in all its manifestations—atom, substance, soul, Form, God), as Nietzsche calls them. Among the ancients the human nervous system had yet to become aware of itself, suspicious of itself. Hence their naivety.

But if no part of the human has not become, if there's no mind or soul independent of, uninfluenced by, the flux of becoming, then there's no guarantee that our sensory-cognitive apparatus tracks anything other than the 'truths' of experience, no guarantee that these 'truths' are true. Life-preserving, yes, but since what's selected for in evolution is success in action, not truth of belief, and since even false beliefs can motivate successful action (i.e., action tending to promote survival and reproduction), survival is no proof of truth. Nietzsche understood this, insisted on it even: 'Life is no argument,' he wrote. 'The conditions of life might include error' (GS 121; compare WP 483, 493). Indeed, untruth is a condition of life, specifically untruth as manifested in those synthetic *a priori* judgments which, according to Kant, are generative of this world of things (in Nietzschean terms, the fiction of enduring things—see BGE 4).

[All of this relates to N's falsificationism, which we discussed a few weeks back. The classic case *against* reading N as a falsificationist in his later period is Clark's *N on Phil and Truth*. Her argument is sufficiently rebutted by Lanier Anderson's review in *Nietzsche-Studien*. Also very good on this topic is Stack's *N's Anthropic Circle*. And maybe it's worth noting here Berry's book on N and ancient skepticism. She takes her case too far, I think. But that's all right. That's just another way of saying that I'm not her.]

Diamythologōmen

So when I speak of the Platonic trust in the senses, I mean to call attention to the fact that one reasons to the Forms by way of taking the world seriously as it presents itself to us, as when in the *Phaedo* one's experience of two sticks launches one on the intellectual path leading eventually to 'insight' into the Form of *equality* (73c-77a: at 74c7-9 Socrates *stresses* that we 'conceive and grasp knowledge of' the Form of *equality* by way of equal particulars, to which Simmias replies with the superlative response formula, *alêthestata*, 'most truly'). But if the world as we experience it—the world of enduring substances, of general natural kinds, etc.—if this world is a phantasm generated by our nervous system as it developed under various survival pressures, then we have reason to be suspicious of the 'truths' we identify in and through it, and even more suspicious of any metaphysical superstructures raised on it as a foundation. Thus Nietzsche himself identifies the belief 'that there are equal things' as one of the erroneous articles of faith at the roots of our 'knowledge.'

Nietzsche traces the error of *being* back to Parmenides, to whose students and followers, the Eleatics, he attributes the invention of the image of the *sage* as one who embodies, intellectually and psychologically, the characteristics of the One (unchanging, impersonal, impassive). He is *being* manifest as man, the light of heaven dwelling on earth. Our own conception of the sage as quiet and serene, still and at peace with himself and the world, with the cosmos even— our notion of the sage descends from the Eleatics and their *being* and their One. But *being* is a fiction, from matter to substance to things to God to the Eleatics' One itself.

Therefore our paradigmatic image of the serious and unperturbable sage is misleading.

For Nietzsche, the man in whom the conflict between the ancient errors of *being* and the insight that *there is only becoming* plays out as an internal intellectual struggle—this man is the 'thinker.' And of course this thinker is the philosopher, the philosopher-artist in the Nietzschean mode. One lesson then of GS 110 is that the philosopher, who revels in the conflict between *being* and *becoming*, who engages in skeptical, innocent, honest, and cheerful intellectual play, and who does all this even as an experiment with life—let's call him a friend of thinking—this type is superior to the sage.

Th, Feb 21

Taking up Socrates' invitation to speak up if he's unsatisfied with the progress of the conversation so far, Simmias proposes an account of the soul as a harmony or attunement of the parts of the body which, if true, would undermine the stipulated separate existence of soul—'soul' would be just a word to designate the fact that the parts and powers of the body function properly together; to think of it as a substance in itself would be a category mistake, as the analytic philosophers like to say.

Socrates meets Simmias's challenge by replying that his soul-as-attunement account is inconsistent with learning as recollection; that if true it would be impossible to understand ignorance or vice in the soul; and that unlike the relation of attunement to an instrument (the attunement exists only through the condition of the instrument, not the other way around), the soul directs and at times even opposes the body.

However successful these remarks may be as objections to Simmias's proposal, they do nothing to prove the still unsupported claim that the soul is separable from the body, much less that it's immortal. Even the last point, which might seem to imply a power distinct from the body, suggests only that something appears sometimes to act contrary to some of the body's impulses, which of course in any particular instance might itself be some other part, aspect, or power of the body. In any case, the point does not demonstrate the existence of soul as a distinct substance.

For all the consternation Simmias's and Cebes' counterarguments caused among Socrates' interlocutors—and even Echecrates declares himself affected—Socrates easily disposes of Simmias's concerns. Cebes' will be more difficult. But we'll get to that. For now I remark on Socrates' urging his friends, despite the difficulties they're encountering in the arguments, not to succumb to misology. There's no greater bad thing one can suffer, he says, than to mistrust *logos* (*ouk estin...hoti an tis meizon toutou kakon pathoi*, 89d2-3). This is a surprising claim, for recall that previously Socrates insisted that being reincarnated without ample time among the gods is the greatest and most extreme of all bad things (*pantôn megiston te kakôn kai eschaton*, 83c2-3).

It's surprising also because it's incongruous with the surrounding content of the dialogue. There's an undercurrent of rebuke in Socrates' warning against misology, as if Simmias and Cebes—and Echecrates and Phaedo too—are at fault, or at risk of being at fault, for their doubts about his reasoning. It might well be a pity to mistrust *logos* if there really is a 'true and certain' argument through which we can acquire 'truth and knowledge of the real,' but Socrates hasn't so far provided any reason to think this likely. He himself has admitted to the gaps and flaws in his reasoning. And the major argument to which all this is preliminary material (his long reply to Cebes' objection) is no better. As we'll see next week, it's utterly dependent on admittedly unproven hypotheses.

Socrates concludes this section by remarking that if what he says (about the immortality of the soul) happens to be true, then it would be admirable (*kalôs*) to believe. Really? Good to believe on the basis of unsound arguments, on insufficient evidence, and on the subjectively determined plausibility of hypotheses and the internal coherence of their apparent implications, because, well, after all, the unsubstantiated conclusion might just *happen* (*tugchanei*) to be true? I'm no evidentialist myself—but that's a matter for another day—but Socrates' position here is far from measuring up to the man's reputation as a 'mystogogue of science,' to employ Nietzsche's formulation. And his remark that even if what he says isn't true, believing it will at least give him peace in the face of death—well, here he admits that his arguments don't really settle anything about the truth of the matter.

If this is the best *logos* can do, or that Socrates can do with *logos*, then I would be reluctant to rebuke any serious thinker who mistrusts it. Could it be that Plato was such a one? The more I read the *Phaedo*, the more I think this might be so. Nothing in the dialogue quite makes sense—not anyway if we mistake it for a straightforward work of what we've been taught to call philosophy.

Tues, Feb 26

Plato can do many things at once, and no doubt he's doing many things in the section recounting Socrates' intellectual biography. Whether this really is Socrates' biography, or Plato's autobiography, or something else altogether—a fiction or semi-fiction—is impossible to determine. Fortunately, this question doesn't concern us. I'm interested in the role this section plays in Socrates' reply to Cebes' complaint that so far he's demonstrated only that the soul is long lasting, but not that it's literally immortal. To make his case for immortality, Socrates will hypothesize the existence of Forms. In this section (95a-107a) he explains his reasons for adopting this approach, develops two different versions of the theory of Forms, and then employs the second version to complete his proof.

I've noted many times by now that Socrates hasn't even attempted to prove the reality of soul as a substance distinct and separable from body. He stipulated this account of soul in his definition of death and he has assumed it throughout. At the end of this section he finally derives soul from other propositions, but it's a dubious derivation—I think of it less as a derivation than a conjuring trick—and anyway it depends utterly on the real existence of Forms, which he stipulates as baldly as earlier he stipulated soul as a separate substance. In the end, then, Socrates shows only that the presumption of soul appears to be consistent with some other ideas taken in a particular way. But he hasn't shown that any of this is true.

Socrates begins by explaining why he abandoned his youthful passion for investigating the causes of things by way of that *sophia* which people call the inquiry into nature (*peri phuseôs historian*). Instead of observing the things themselves, he says, he now takes refuge in (*kataphugonta*: lit, he flees down into) *logoi* (96a-100a). What this means is none too clear, but at a minimum it means, as Socrates explains, that when thinking about cause and everything else, he hypothesizes the *logos* which he judges most formidable (*errômenestaton*, which has the primary meaning of physical vigor), and he postulates as true those things that harmonize with it. We might say he trusts the judgment of his subjectivity as to what's plausible and then investigates the implications. In the present context he proposes to hypothesize Forms, and if Cebes will grant him these, and concede that they exist, he hopes to demonstrate that the soul is immortal (100a-b). Cebes for his part does not hesitate to grant Socrates his hypothesis.

Yet despite securing Cebes' agreement, Socrates again explains his resorting to hypotheses and says, in effect, that he will not entertain any objections to the existence of Forms—that would necessitate an altogether different conversation (101c-e). But Socrates' determination simply to hypothesize Forms doesn't worry his interlocutors at all. In fact, they're so satisfied with his methodology that they simultaneously reply with the enthusiastically affirmative response formula, 'You speak most truly' (*alethestata... legeis*, 102a2: this is the only instance in the dialogue of both

Simmias and Cebes employing this superlative response formula to one and the same idea). And here too Phaedo and Echecrates reappear to approve Socrates' method, with Phaedo particularly stressing that the reality of Forms was conceded and agreed to (102a10-b2).

All this is to say that Plato has made a point of stressing that Socrates offers no demonstration whatever of the foundational premise of his argument. Evidently he intends to focus his reader's mind on what Socrates is up to here, namely, he has secured his interlocutors' permission to assume the reality of Forms and so to ground his final 'proof' on an utterly unsubstantiated proposition.

We need not dwell on the details of Socrates' demonstration. Suffice it to say that, according to Socrates' original theory of Forms (which at 105b-c he calls safe but ignorant [*amathê*]), the presence of (the Form of) *life* in a thing would cause it to be alive, but on his modified theory (also safe, but more refined or ingenious—*kompsoteran*), *life* is something like an essential property of soul, and soul is that which when present in a body causes it to be alive. In short, from his 'other safe' version of the theory of Forms Socrates conjures soul as something like a vehicle for, or carrier of, *life*. He then argues that since life is an essential property of soul, soul will never admit the presence of the opposite of life, namely death. Therefore, the soul is deathless, and since the deathless is also indestructible, the soul will not dissolve and disperse when the body dies. Therefore, Socrates concludes, our souls after death really will be in Hades (*tôi onti esontai hêmôn hai psychai en Haidou*, 107a1).

This last formulation recalls the beginning of Socrates' defense of his defense, which commenced after Cebes remarked that his defense might be persuasive if our souls endure after the death of the body (see in particular the formulation, *en Haidou eisin hai psychai*) (70a-c).

Cebes is convinced by Socrates' argument. Simmias for his part says that he has no way to dispute the *logos*, but he adds that he does retain some doubt (*apsitia*) given the magnitude of the subject and his disdain for human weakness.

Perhaps somewhat surprisingly, Socrates not only affirms Simmias's skeptical reservations, he even adds that the first hypotheses of his argument (i.e., Forms) must be investigated further, even if they find them credible. Not on this day, but in general, for all these arguments amount to nothing if the hypothesis on which they're based is false. So it seems that even Socrates understands that he hasn't really demonstrated anything beyond the apparent consistency of a set of propositions. Whether the propositions, besides being mutually consistent, are true—this is another question, and to answer it would require, at least, a demonstration of the reality of Forms. And it's not even clear that Socrates thinks there's any such demonstration available. It may be that the most we can hope to do is follow the *logos* as thoroughly as it's possible for a human to follow it. Beyond this, he says, there is nothing to be sought (107b).

In sum, then, Socrates' final argument for the immortality of soul simply hypothesizes Forms, then conjures soul from Forms plus the 'other safe answer,' namely that soul is a vehicle for (the Form of) *life* rather than just *life* alone being that which when present in a body makes it living. Nothing else about the soul has been demonstrated; not even, for example, that it is conscious. To secure the soul as intelligent and moral requires, at least, recollection and virtue-as-purification and/or reincarnation, both of which are simply assumed throughout (so it's not just the bare existence of Forms that Socrates hypothesizes, but much else besides). In short, the entire edifice is built on unproven hypotheses. Perhaps this is why the defense of Socrates' defense amounts in the end to a *mythos*.

Th, Feb 28

There's no need to examine the details of Socrates' account of the afterlife, the underworld, and the true earth. Not for our purposes anyway. But there are some elements of this section that are relevant to our investigations. [The chapters on the *Phaedo* myth in Kingsley's *Ancient Phil, Mystery, and Magic* are well worth reading for detailed information on all this.]

Notice that Socrates' account of the fate of the soul immediately after death—its being met by a *daimôn* and led into the underworld—is based on what 'is said' (*legetai*) and on popular 'rituals and customs.' Then, when he speaks of the shape of the earth, he stresses (four times) that he's been 'persuaded by someone' of the information. And later he introduces his account of 'the realities on the earth under heaven'—which includes the judgment and rewards and punishments of souls—by saying that he will *mython legein*, or speak a myth (110b1), to which Simmias replies that they will gladly hear 'this myth' (110b3-4). Finally, when Socrates concludes, he remarks (and here I translate quite literally), 'To confidently affirm that these things are as I have recounted is not fitting for a man with an intellect' (114d1-2), then he repeats his description of these things as a *mythos* (114d7).

So what are we left with in the end? Not certainty, that's for sure. Not even probability. It seems there's only the great hope which Socrates mentions at the conclusion of his myth (*hê elpis megalê*, 114c9). That's a meager result for so long a conversation. Perhaps that's why, after admitting that no man of intellect would insist on the accuracy of what he's said, Socrates obfuscates with the following convoluted sentence: 'That these things [I've just gone through] are so, or that some such things about our souls and [their] dwellings [are so], since really the soul appears to be immortal, this, it seems to me, is both fitting and worth the risk to one thinking it to be this way—for the risk is noble—and it is necessary that he sing such things to himself as an incantation' (114d2-7).

The soul *appears* to be immortal, he says. That's a feeble claim. And yet, weak as it is, it's still too bold for what the *logos* has actually come to. Does Socrates imagine that his lengthy intervening *mythos* about the underworld has made everyone forget that he himself acknowledged (at 107b) that their 'first hypotheses, even if they're credible to us, should be examined more distinctly'? That's quite a lot remaining to examine. I suppose that until we've managed that, all we have really *is* just an incantation.

Diamythologōmen

So, we've seen that Socrates doesn't prove the immortality of the soul, much less any of his other assertions about its nature, either in this or in the supposed next life. If we don't believe anteriorly in Forms, and various associated dogma (like the idea that learning is recollection), then Socrates hasn't rendered any of his claims even probable. It's all a *mythos*, a charm (recall 77d-78a), a raft on which to sail through the dangers of life (85c-d), or the prophetic vapors of a doomed man who fancies himself a co-servant with the swans of Apollo (84d-85b).

As I've said before, one wonders what's really going on here. Put it this way: why exactly did Plato write this dialogue? Apparently not to prove that the soul is immortal. Not only does he not prove this, everyone involved in the conversation is well aware that Socrates hasn't completed a proof—not least because he himself points this out, insists on it even. The arguments throughout are weak, and their flaws are noted either by Simmias and Cebes or by Socrates himself. The gravest problem with much of the *logos* is that it simply stipulates the existence of a separable soul. And when Socrates delivers his final argument, through which he finally derives the soul's existence as a substance independent of the body, he does so by way of yet another stipulation, namely Forms, and a particular variation on the operation of Forms (the 'other safe' version of his theory). It's a conjuring trick. Really, just as he conjures soul from the need to have a vehicle to carry (the Form of) *life* into the body, so he conjures his doctrine worth the risk of believing from a hodgepodge of myths and dubious arguments.

But to return to my question. Why did Plato write this dialogue? Why compose such a long and intricate work that, considered solely with respect to its central *logos*, takes something like the following form: 'This fictional character persuades these other fictional characters to accept claims, or to be comforted by claims, or at least to stop objecting to claims, which they all admit to be unjustified, or to be justified only on the assumption of a doctrine, and several other attendant claims, which none of these fictional characters provide either themselves or you, reader, any good reason to believe.'

I won't try to answer this question in full. But I will say again that it seems to me that Plato did *not* write the *Phaedo* to prove that the soul is immortal. Nor even to offer us readers consolation when confronted by death in our own lives. Really, where's the consolation in an unsubstantiated doctrine which can be commended solely on the grounds that to believe it is a noble risk?

Tues, March 5

Recall Nietzsche's account of the dying Socrates in *The Birth of Tragedy* as the paradigmatic theoretical man, the optimistic dialectician tranquil in the face of death. In *The Gay Science*, Nietzsche stresses instead the significance of Socrates' last words, which he interprets as a condemnation of life. Socrates' obligation to sacrifice to Asclepius, the god of healing, suggests to Nietzsche that Socrates regarded his life as a sickness, for which death was the cure. Socrates suffered from life, and despite his apparently cheerful demeanor, he had in fact been a pessimist.

Diamythologōmen

Nietzsche makes the same point in *Twilight of the Idols*, adding that Socrates' 'weariness of life,' even 'resistance to life,' is evidence of Socrates' decadence. Socrates—and Plato too—were 'pseudo-Greek, anti-Greek.'

Socrates may well have been decadent, and Nietzsche provides many reasons to affirm this—for example, the 'anarchy of his instincts' and the 'hypertrophy of [his] logical faculty' (this from TI); but if the *Phaedo* doesn't really teach the possibility of escape from the cycle of rebirth, then we can't count this as one among his legitimate indictments of the man. (At 95c-d Socrates seems to imply that embodied life is *not* a sickness—see specifically the *nosos* at 95d2.) Rather, we should stress Socrates' status as the 'mystagogue of science' who privileged soul over body, reason over instinct, Apollo over Dionysus. We could add 'radical ascetic,' though from the totality of evidence it's not clear whether this is a fair description of Socrates the man or only of the character in the *Phaedo*.

In any case, even if we join Nietzsche in condemning Socrates on these grounds, I'm confident that we can't include Plato in the indictment. Let's agree that Socrates exaggerated the power and significance of *logos*. Fine. But we can't say the same about Plato, and it seems to me that the *Phaedo* itself provides ample evidence of this. At every turn the *logos* is subverted by, diverted toward, or transformed into *mythos*. And taking the dialogue as a whole, the *logos* (such as it is) is but one element of a broader *mythos*. And of course we can't—we *shouldn't*—forget that Plato himself has staged all this. Plato the philosopher-artist. Plato who, to remind you, Nietzsche once wrote, *used*

Notes on Plato and Nietzsche

Socrates as an 'audacious interpreter' picks up a popular tune to 'vary it into the infinite and impossible—namely, into all of his own masks and multiplicities.'

Why would Plato use Socrates this way? Why would *we* want to cast their relationship in these terms? We've discussed the fact that Plato lived and practiced philosophy quite differently from Socrates, and we might suppose he had an interest in advocating his personal approach by subtly contrasting it with Socrates' version of the philosophical life. That's reasonable, it seems to me; and it's consistent with our reading of the *Phaedo* [with other dialogues too—for example, Plato's condemnation of the misuse of dialectic in *Republic* 7 reads very much like a criticism of Socratic practice; also telling is the fact that Socratic dialectic fails to dissuade Euthyphro from prosecuting his father despite it's being evident from the details of the case that he's in the wrong—as Nietzsche wrote in TI, dialectic arouses mistrust and isn't really persuasive].

As to our own motivations, I want to suggest that by underscoring the differences between Plato and Socrates *as philosophers* we might at last liberate ourselves from Socrates and ally ourselves instead with Plato; we might stand with the private ~~thinker-artist~~ friend of thinking against the public dialectician. As a character within the work, Socrates represents doctrine. Plato as the author represents the creative thinking-life of philosophy.

And speaking of the *Republic*, we should keep in mind that Plato is not the teacher of dialectic imagined in Book 6 of that work; he is rather the *author* of the book—an altogether different type. And we don't aspire to be teachers of dialectic any more than we want to be scholars or disciples of philosophical dogma. We want to become philosophers ourselves, and toward this end, I think—no, I've *found*, in my own thinking life—I've found it helps to distance Plato from Socrates and align him rather with Nietzsche, philosopher-artist with philosopher-artist.

Th, March 7

So what to make of the *Phaedo*? What *is* it, exactly? It's a work of philosophy. Ok, but philosophy as...what? As *logos*, as *mythos*, as a *mythos-logos* or *diamythologomena*—things discussed by way of mythologizing?

Let's revisit our realization that the dialogue doesn't teach the possibility of permanent escape from the cycle of rebirth. This is not what the properly purified philosopher is after. So what does he want? He wants a long afterlife. The hope is to avoid falling back into a body too soon. Socrates wants to spend time with the gods, which is to say among the Forms, because only thus will he be reborn as a human, and the more knowledge he acquires while communing with the Forms the more likely it is he'll be reborn as a human *philosopher*. Socrates wants to ensure that his next incarnation not be as a donkey, a wolf, or even a social animal like a bee, in which form men are born who are temperate and just but without philosophical understanding (80b-82b). And of course he doesn't want to come back as just any type of man, a tyrant, say, or a blacksmith. No, Socrates hopes that when he returns he'll live precisely the sort of life he lived this time around, which is to say a philosophical life.

But that's Socrates, as a character in Plato's dialogue. I'm not convinced that Plato himself was committed to either reincarnation or the metaphysical apparatus associated with it. Why not? To begin with, there's the fact that he constantly undermines Socrates' arguments, exposing them as unsound at worst or as internally consistent but unproven at best. As I said on Tuesday, he's always working Socrates' *logoi* over into his own *mythos*.

There's also this. Recall Simmias's remark, following Socrates' last argument, that although he has no grounds to doubt what's been said, he still lacks belief due to the magnitude of the subject and 'human weakness' (107a-b). The word for weakness here is *astheneia*, and in the *Phaedo* it's associated with doubting, or failing to comprehend, the reality of the metaphysical. The latter association appears when Socrates attributes our inability to attain 'the true heaven, the true light, the true earth' to *astheneia*, precisely as this same condition prevents his imagined sea dwellers from knowing our realm above the waters (109b-110a). This word, *astheneia*, is associated also with the body as opposed to the soul (as at 87a and 87d-e).

I go into these details because, as I trust you remember, Plato isn't present for the conversation because '*êsthenei*,' which is to say he was suffering from *astheneia*. And this suggests to me that Plato means to align himself with those like Simmias who waver between belief and unbelief when it comes to the metaphysics of the *Phaedo*, and who value the body and embodied life in a way the characters in this radically ascetic dialogue apparently can't imagine.

Diamythologōmen

So, as I say, I'm not convinced that Plato was committed to the metaphysics of the soul and the afterlife which Socrates defends in the *Phaedo*. As a character in the dialogue, Socrates is a literalist about these things; as author, Plato is writing figuratively. Plato agrees with Socrates that the life of the philosopher is the highest life, but he disagrees as to what exactly this entails. The authentic philosopher lives philosophy constantly, lives and loves it so thoroughly that he (or she) would even choose to philosophize forever, were that really possible. Plato's Socrates may hope that it is, but Plato evidently disagrees.

In short, then, as to the substance of the *Phaedo*: Socrates' desire literally to return to life in the future as a philosopher is Plato's mythologized affirmation of the philosophical life, here and now.

[John Burnet contended that the idea of a separable conscious soul originated with Socrates, and that Plato inherited the doctrine of Forms from him too, it being a Pythagorean teaching. I'm suggesting that we take Burnet's insight one step further: not only did Plato not invent these ideas—he had recurring radical doubts about the whole scheme.]

So what's up with the *Phaedo*? The honest answer is, as with every question about Plato, *I don't know*. But I will say this. The *Phaedo* is a work of philosophy, no doubt. But philosophy not as *logos*, nor even exactly as *mythos*. Rather, to recall a word I mentioned earlier, adapted from the *Phaedo* itself, it's philosophy as *diamythologomena*. That is to say, it's a sprawling, dense, deep, rich, complex work of philosophical art, a compendium of ideas and images, *logoi*

and *mythoi*, of assertions and contradictions, of arguments, puzzles, mysteries, and profundities, dreams, fantasies, musings, theories, intimations and provocations—and all this for the sake of thinking, for thinking as exploration, as experimentation, as overabundance, as spirit, as play, as life. In short, and to employ a Platonic formulation, we can call the *Phaedo* a philosophical-artistic production of *theia mania*. In Nietzsche's terms, *die fröhliche Wissenschaft, la gaya scienza*.
...

For next week: free-form discussion on Plato and Nietzsche, both days. On Thursday assign the preface to *The Gay Science* for after spring break.

Primavera

"Scialla! Sciaaallaaa! Sei sveglia, Sciallina? Oh, sì, eccoti! Buongiorno! Hai dormito bene? Sì? Brava! Brava, Sciallina!

"Guarda, Scialla, look outside—it's spring! The first day of spring! La primavera! Guarda! Il tempo è bello, no? Il sole, il cielo. Sì, sì, che bello! La primavera, Scialla! Veramente! Finalmente!

"Va bene, Scialla. Facciamo un giro? Around the block? Andiamo? Sì, dai, let's go!"

...

The silence, ah, yes, the early morning hush. Listen. Nothing. No one. Only the glittering dew-dropped spiderwebs, serene repose, the quiet calm awakening. Spring. I'll miss the winter chill when I'm sweating in the *caldo cattivo* this summer in Italy, but for now, *proprio adesso*, the equipollence of the equinox, the atmospheric tranquility—Ha! Twice a year even the earth itself's a Pyrrhonian!

"Vero, Scialla? Il mondo a Pyrrhonian. Equinoctial equipollence, cosmic *ataraxia*. Ha! Una bella fantasia, no?"

Una bella fantasia, davvero.

Fantasy, the fantastical cartographer. Creek and cloud. Thought and world. The *regressus ad infinitum*.

Oh, but—

Basta! Don't think about the book.

But I can think about the book without thinking *for* the book. It's a book for *thinking*, after all.

Yeah, but let's just walk...

...

Primavera

How does one live philosophy as a free-spirit?

But you're always asking this. So how about this: Stop asking how to do it, and just do it.

Yes, but do what, exactly?

Live philosophy free-spiritedly.

Yes, but what's that?

You're asking me what it is to live philosophy as a free-spirit?

Yes.

I don't know.

Exactly!

...

'To walk along on a lonely street is part of the philosopher's nature.' He had himself in mind there too, no doubt. As do I.

There. The spread of trees. Verdant field of colors, multi-hued, overlapping, stacked and interlaced, all along this lonely street. Field of vision, colors of nature. 'The rural places and the trees.'

I've been watching—*we've* been watching. "Vero, Scialla?" Walking and watching. Walking thinking and observing. The shrubs bloomed first, Lilac and Forsythia, purple-pink and blazing yellow. (Forsythia, right?) Two or three weeks back. The trees a little later. The Star Magnolia (great song!), followed by the Bradford Pear ('Cut Down Bradford Pears'), then the Redbud, then the Cherry, and now the delicate Dogwoods. Delicate Dogwoods, pink and white. And jade-green lawns, dive in.

"Sì, Scialla! Gioca, gioca! Brava, Scialla! Gioca! —op, aspetta! Aspetta, Scialla. Vieni qua. Siediti. Sit, Scialla, sit.

Sì, così. Brava... Morning. Fine, thanks... Brava! Brava, Sciallina! Sempre lui, vero? Always that guy."

Ha! Probably thinking the same thing about me. But you know, it's pleasant, here in the south, that people smile and say hello. It's silly to pass a man shoulder to shoulder and behave as if you don't notice, or you're too distracted to acknowledge fellow-feeling at least with a nod.

And in the freshness of an early spring morning a leafy American neighborhood is in its way a rival to any place in Europe, blooming lush and fragrant, a hymn to future life, floral fugue, nature's affirmation of abundance.

And come to think of it, you do have a good idea what it is to live philosophy as a free-spirit. Divine madness. *La gaya scienza*. Creative-Pyrrhonism and the thinker-artist. (The friend of thinking.)

But how do I know this account's correct?

But now you're after certainty, which is contrary to the account.

Right, but essentially it's a variety of skepticism, or playful non-commitment, so naturally I'm dubious even of the account itself. It's necessarily self-reflective, and therefore maybe also self-refuting.

Like you. Ha! But, well, maybe without insisting on the *necessarily*, in the strict sense anyway. Skepticism with regard to reason and all that, right? And self-refuting goes too far.

Yeah, ok. But what exactly does this free-spirited philosophical life *look* like, in action? If I don't know that, I'll never know whether I'm really living it. So, for example, am I living the life right now, walking and thinking these thoughts? Was I living it last week, discussing these ideas in class in the context of Plato and Nietzsche?

Well, yes. Thinking these thoughts in this way—doing what I'm doing now—this is the free-spirited, creative-pyrrhonian, thinker-artist's life. Especially thinking these thoughts toward a larger project which aims to be a creative work of philosophy. The book.

(Don't think about the book. Just think.)

Conversations. Philosophical Conversations.

It's a book for thinking, so, taking long walks, and spending time alone or in my head—solitude in the Nietzschean sense—and in that time reflecting on traditional philosophical themes—being and becoming; the one and the many; knowledge and skepticism; objectivism and subjectivity—the fundamental questions, or anyway the questions a man of my psychological and intellectual disposition tends to regard as fundamental. Is there a really real? If so, what's it like, and can we know it? If not, is there anything else, and can that be known?

The philosopher as the friend of thinking and philosophy as a way of life. To—

Oh, hey, look at this! The new owners are meticulous about their yard. A little garden even. "Guarda, Scialla, guarda! I fiori son' belli, vero? Sì! Beautiful flowers!" Ha! Well, the neighbors must be delighted.

And not only thinking about these subjects, but thinking with reference to canonical figures—Plato, Nietzsche, Hume, Quine, Rorty—and with a scholar's knowledge of the relevant primary and secondary literature. So in a sense this manifestly is a philosophical life, even academic. But then the specific collection of these thoughts—the art of selecting these and just these ideas, and arranging and interweaving them in this and not some other way, and with this as opposed to a different end in view—and the attention to the prose, to style, and the variety of modes of composition—all this, thinking the thoughts (the primary thing) and expressing them just so in writing—all this is the free-spirited element.

So:

Living – philosophy – free-spiritedly

is

thinking – about philosophy – in this way.

Walking; thinking; about these subjects; in this way; regularly. Yes. This is the free-spirited, creative-pyrrhonian, thinker-artist's life. The friend of thinking, and philosophy as a way of life.

And this I think is similar to—similar *at a minimum*—to Nietzsche's notion of the free-spirit as a philosophical type. Moreover, it takes seriously what's possible for philosophy after Nietzsche. Once it's all been undermined, from morality to truth, from the self to God, what's left to argue?

Play! Not frivolously though; these matters are no less serious than they've always been.

And I take this conception of philosophy to descend from Plato too—Plato the philosopher, the creative thinker and writer; not Platonism as doctrine. The man, not the dialogues. The artist, not the art. And for myself I want primarily to be an artist, a philosopher-artist, only secondarily to 'understand' someone else's philosophical art.

Anyway this is what philosophy as a way of life *should* be. Not *to study Plato* (or Nietzsche) but *to become a Plato* (or a Nietzsche), which is to say to live the thinking life. This involves the study of texts and doctrine, but much more than this besides (Art!), more than mastering arguments and details. Much more again than mastering the secondary sources, which is valuable too in moderation, of course, but in excess it distracts one from philosophy. It's a student's, a scholar's, or a disciple's way of life—the life of a Platonist, not a Plato.

Ha! Makes me think of grad school, where philosophy goes to die. The cold wards of intellect-surgeons who specialize in removing the *fröhliche* from the *Wissenschaft*. Ha!

...

"Come va, Scialla? Tutto bene? Sei brava? Sì, come sempre. Sei bravissima!"

Not to study but to be. Of course I value 'getting Plato right,' but I have a greater interest in using Plato to do what's right for me.

Self-creation.

It's worth the risk. It's worth the risk of believing something wrong or antiquated—or of doubting something 'obviously' right or good—or of being 'on the wrong side of history'—Ha! That's precisely where I want to be!—it's worth the risk to escape the prison-house of contemporary and contingent prejudices, intellectual and spiritual—*kalos gar ho kindunos*!

Today this applies particularly to social, political, and cultural dogma, which is everywhere forced on one's attention. Party politics. But I'm not now concerned with trivialities and diversions from *my own way*.

It's like Nietzsche on the study of the Greeks as 'a means to *understand ourselves*, to judge our time, and thereby to overcome it.' Yes! To overcome one's time! To lay the skin of centuries between oneself and the present day! The philosopher as a free-spirit, as *really* free, should break the chains of every contemporary prejudice. Ah, that we're everywhere in chains is true *especially* of our *intellect*.

Personally, I have no particular interest in my time, nor in preserving the cultural conditions that make philosophy possible, the Straussians' preoccupation. So Lampert cites Nietzsche in a political mood, 'What matters to me is *the preservation of my kind!!*—' This makes no sense to me. Why exactly should this matter, above all else? The activities required to preserve the philosopher as a type—the political engagement—generally contradict, inhibit, or distract one from the activities required to live as a philosopher oneself. If the philosopher's central task were to generate future philosophers, the philosopher would be no better than the ant, breeding solely to produce new breeders. No, the central task is thinking, for oneself, as oneself.

Why not? One can be indifferent to contemporary politics—even actively opposed to participating—without being morbidly-ascetically obsessed with the state of one's own soul. Political activism rots the brain. Maybe I'd judge differently if the issue were archaic Hellenism, Nietzsche's subject, the Pre-Platonic philosopher-statesman's drive to preserve Hellenic culture, but today there's no culture worth preserving, nor any hope of cultural regeneration. I suppose we can forgive a nineteenth-century naivety—especially in an excitable youth seduced by Wagner's mythopoeic genius—but no more. Political engagement today is only harmful, a distraction with no benefits, or anyway none sufficient to override the harm.

What matters to me is *to be a friend of thinking!!*—

...

But philosophy doesn't bake bread! they say.

Yeah, yeah, we've heard all that before. The refrain of the politician, the administrator, the bureaucrat. Philistines.

Should I reply that man doesn't live by bread alone?

Each side has its evidence and arguments. These days I just do as I please. *Think* as I please. I don't pray for Reality's blessing with an offering of arguments. Justification by faith in Truth. Divine Truth. I trust the judgment of my subjectivity.

I know, having thought and having observed myself think for many years now, that *this* is where my thoughts tend to go when *this* subject comes up. Eternalism, for example. And that's enough for me. Do I believe it? To be true? But what's this supposed to mean, exactly? What's it add? That I have evidence in my pocket, or a sound argument? That I'll 'defend it against all comers'? That I'm pledged to stick with it—that I have reasons that *oblige* me to stick with it? I have plenty to say 'in defense' of what I think, if you want to put it that way. I just don't find that way of putting it particularly helpful.

Belief, knowledge, truth. It's all just so much handwaving. My thinking life is its own justification. The defense of philosophy as good in itself and for its own sake (as

Aristotle's *theôria*, for example)—it's a pretty thought, but quaint. It's a mask. It's a mask disguising, 'I enjoy it; I like to think about these things in this way.'

Philosophy as the higher hedonism!

Right! Objectivism is the mask insecurity wears over subjectivity.

And the mask speaks. It says: 'It's not me; it's the world.'

Ha! Exactly! So let's just admit it. "Vero, Scialla?" Let's be frank. There is no proof. There's just me.

We have as options *yes* and *no*, *true* and *false*, *good* and *bad*. But we're not satisfied with only *yes* or *no*. We insist that our *yes* follows from *true* or *good*, our *no* from *false* or *bad*. Thus we shift responsibility for our Yea or Nay from our subjectivity onto the world, some property of reality in itself. We call this 'justification,' and justification takes precedence over explanation, which is to say in this case self-revelation. 'This is why it's *right* that I believe this,' we say. 'This is why it's *good* that I do this.' Rarely do we admit the simple fact, 'This is *who I am*.'

We want to believe our affirmations are acceptable, to others besides ourselves. To our peers; to the experts; to reality; to God. But the very idea of objective truth might be incoherent, or otherwise illegitimate. And even granting that it makes sense, we have no idea whether there's any such thing, or, if there is, how to go about knowing it, or whether knowing it is better than not. —Oh, rabbits!

"No, Scialla, no! Stai calma now. They're not food. Vieni qua. Stai calma."

...

Primavera

The practical function of the concept *truth* is to reconcile us to our perspectival subjectivity. 'I'm justified in believing or doing or feeling such and such because it's true, and thereby do I align with the real, and thereby am I good. The universe approves. I'm ok.'

But for a thoughtful mind the question marks go all the way down. To demand proof, to need truth, is a weakness of the spirit. We just don't know, never will. So don't stress about the truth. (Everything is permitted!) Affirm the activity of a refined subjectivity. Do this, or suffer.

Ok, but be specific. What is it that I really want? Richness of experience, intellectual independence, psychological exploration, depth of insight, creative activity, affirmative cheerfulness. Good by my own lights.

Philosophy as the higher hedonism. I'd say the *highest*, but that would be the mask speaking.

...

All right, see? There, like that. Thinking *those* thoughts in *that* way. What I've just been doing, *that's* the philosophical life—that, which is to say, *this*.

Ok. But if all this really is what I should be doing, and if I really am doing it—and I've been telling myself for years now that it *is*, and that I *am*—if so, then why the wavering, uncertainty, and anxiety? Why the compulsion to revisit the same questions: Is the free-spirited, creative-pyrrhonian, thinker-artist's life the authentic or supreme expression of philosophy? And is *this*, what I'm doing now—is this it? Am I living it? Why not finally resolve these questions, with a Yes!, in my head as in my rhetoric? Get on with living the life.

Well, but maybe constantly returning to the questions, sorting anew through every answer, the self-reflective loop—maybe this is part of the life.

Ha! I hope so, because that's precisely what I'm doing now. But seriously, I worry that maybe the infinite self-reflectivity is infinitely self-undermining.

Yes, well, but you know, it may also be self-fortifying. Why not? You don't have to lose yourself in the infinite regress. You can find yourself there too. It's all you, after all. Me.

It's like Plato and the *Phaedo*. He associates himself with skepticism by way of weakness, *astheneia*, but as the stronger comes to be from the weaker, and the weaker from the stronger, in an endless cycle of transformations, so Plato cycles back and forth between belief and doubt, realism and skepticism.

So maybe it doesn't stop. Maybe there's no end, and maybe that's a *good thing*.

The problem is you're accustomed to thinking under the aspect of melancholy, often even intentionally summoning the mood. You contemplate a mountain view, a shaded wood, or a field of flowers, and you score your experience with wistful melodies, autumnal harmonies. Nostalgia. Why not stand before the scene and think your thoughts to a joyful tune? Affirmative cheerfulness, as you say. The thoughts are only thoughts, after all. They're not moods in and of themselves, nor are they necessarily conjoined with any particular emotion. So alter the association.

Think of it as an emotional change of aspect, a mood shift, on the model of Wittgenstein's duck-rabbit. The mood-aspect appears to be encoded in the scene, but it's not, not exclusively, and you can change the aspect. You want to experiment? Experiment with that.

Oh, ok, I like that. Write that down.

But we're not thinking about the book.

No, no, we're not. I'm just thinking. And here's the thought. If philosophy really is the higher hedonism, let's squeeze some joy out of it!

...

Conversations. Conversations, or *Philosophical Conversations*? Yeah, that's better. Anyway it's more descriptive. But considering all the spirals, loops, and self-reflectivity, the substance and the imagery, maybe 'reflections' is better still. *Philosophical Reflections*. It's evocative of the mirror. Alright, sure, but probably it's too obvious.

But don't think about the book. Just think.

But I *am* just thinking. The book just happens to be my subject.

It's a book for *thinking*, nothing else.

The friend of thinking, cheerfully keeping company with creative thinking.

Nine chapters in three triads, and overall a ring composition. First triad: thinking, teaching, imaginative dialogue (a, b, c); second triad: the dialogue moves up one spot for: thinking, dialogue, teaching (a, c, b); third triad: the dialogue moves up again, to first position, and the next two switch positions for: dialogue, teaching, thinking (c, b, a). A ring of an ennead.

A *ring of an ennead*? Oh, now that I like. Remember that.

Diamythologōmen

Ok, yeah. So the chapter now titled 'Varia' rework into a style to triplet with the *creek and cloud* and *regressus* chapters, and rename it. And for the Plato and Nietzsche chapter, maybe revise my *Phaedo* notes from class. But I should do that soon, while it's all still fresh in mind. The final thinking chapter with Scialla again, in the spring, as a conclusion to the book.

"Va bene, Scialla? I'll write about you again. Perché sei brava, vero? Sì, anche allegra, felice ed allegra. I should learn from you, Scialla, vero? Learn from you about high-spirits and cheerfulness. Brava! Sì! Brava, Sciallina!"

So the book's about reality, the possibility of knowledge, the value of the will to truth, and the philosophical life. Also the psychology, emotions, anxieties, and activities of a thinker thinking about all this. And thinking about all of *this*. So not just the conclusions but the thinking itself—the life in which the thoughts are thought and the various modes of expressing the thoughts—as wandering reflections, as teaching, as dialogue, or as *the book itself*.

It's also a portrayal of a *particular type* of philosophy, of the philosopher as the free-spirited, creative-pyrrhonian thinker-artist. The friend of thinking. And written in that mode. The style should enact the substance.

So the book's a philosophical portrait of a philosopher philosophizing.

It's a philosopher reflected in the mirror of his mind.

Really, it's a *self-portrait*.

Oh, hey, I like all that. A self-portrait. Remember that. A philosophical portrait of a philosopher philosophizing. Yeah, write that down.

But I foresee a certain type of reader who won't be able to resist objecting to my 'arguments.' That's fine, I suppose. I can't compel anyone to take the book as I intend it, nor do I want to. But I would like to reply: I'm not arguing for a conclusion. I'm articulating a perspective. I'm just sharing what I think. For example, if I say, or imply, 'If x, then y,' this isn't necessarily an assertion that y is deducible from x. Sometimes it might be, but more likely it indicates only that in my own mind, when I think x I tend also to think y. It's a psychological or conceptual association, only some small part of which is based on inference or deduction. Or I guess the percentage differs depending on the subject or my mood. In any case, there's no need to get worked up about it. No call to be contentious. I don't want to argue about it. I'm just thinking out loud. And surely we don't have to think alike, all of us, cramped in the same perspective. Let's let one another be, each to his own way of thinking, especially if we're familiar with the relevant positions and arguments. If we know the score. I know the score.

I suppose it's the difference between philosophy regarded as the intellectual activity of rationally demonstrating the truth of a systematic collection of assertoric propositions, and philosophy as thinking, sometimes out loud.

And I'm just thinking out loud. Right. I'm recounting, elaborating, displaying the movement of my thought. I don't mean to suggest that it's the *truth*, even though now and then I assert this or that, appeal to evidence, or formulate arguments myself. The train of thought is manifest in many forms. Its occasional configuration as an argument, as a syllogism, is just one of many conduits through which the thought is transmitted, a disposable body to objectify the spirit of the thought, temporarily. It's a mode of expression, and not at all a privileged mode. The *logos* is just one component of a more expansive *mythos*.

Anyway, the point is that I don't insist on belief, mine or anyone else's. Epistemic obligation or compulsion by reason. Belief's really up to each individual subjectivity. I'll recommend my musings to the reader as additions to his store of thoughts and perspectives, nothing more.

"Ah, Scialla, it's a shame I can't discuss these thoughts with you. You're happy but you're no philosopher. You don't even read. Ha! But you play, vero? Sì, giochi, giochi davvero! Every day. E tu *ami* la vita! And that's the thing Scialla, that's the thing! To love life with exuberance, to think and laugh and dream and play. I really can learn from you, Scialla. Brava! Brava, Sciallina!"

So the book's a point of view elaborated, and the idea, or the hope, is that the substance of the point of view and the various modes of elaboration will entertain, exhilarate, infuriate, inspire, mystify, move, provoke, or evoke reverie or insight or pleasure in the reader's heart, mind, or spirit.

And the imperative of the book is not: Read and believe! It's rather: Read, explore, enjoy, and—*think!*

...

"Oh, guarda lì, Scialla! La nostra casa, vedi?"
Home!

THE END

www.ingramcontent.com/pod-product-compliance
Lightning Source LLC
Chambersburg PA
CBHW030436010526
44118CB00011B/657